LMS
Branch Lines
❧ England and Wales ❧

The Midland scene, summertime at Upton-on Severn with 3F No 43337 and one coach train on 8 August 1953. A Midland gas lamp can be seen to the right, Midland chairs hold the bull head rails, and a "Hawkseye" nameboard, placed at an angle, complete the picture. The line closed to passengers on 14 August 1961, and freight on 1 July 1963. Photograph by N. Glover.

LMS
Branch Lines

❧ England and Wales ❧

C. J. Gammell

OPC

Oxford Publishing Co.

A catalogue record for this book is available from the British Library

ISBN 0-86093-498-5

Oxford Publishing Co. is part of the
Haynes Publishing Group
Sparkford, Near Yeovil, Somerset. BA22 7JJ

Haynes Publications Inc.
861 Lawrence Drive, Newbury Park, California 91320, USA.

Printed by: J.H. Haynes & Co. Ltd

CONTENTS

Tal-y-cafn station on the former LNWR Blaenau Ffestiniog branch is one of the few traditionally run country stations left on BR. The station is staffed, as the crossing gates have to be manned. The station still has a well kept garden.

An LMS branch line preserved, 8F 2-8-0 No 8431 arrives at Oxenhope on the Keighley & Worth Valley Railway. The station is restored to BR, London Midland Region colours of the 1950s.

PREFACE

The London Midland & Scottish Railway existed from 1923 until 1947 and was the largest company in Britain. The railway even claimed to be the largest company in the world. The employees amounted to nearly ¼-million people and the capital value of the company was over £400 million. The LMS was a vast organisation and included the former London & North Western Railway, the Midland, Lancashire & Yorkshire, Glasgow & South Western, Caledonian, North Stafford, and Highland Railways amongst its constituents.

The LMS became in main the London Midland Region of the nationalised British Railways in 1948, the territory north of Carlisle becoming incorporated into the Scottish Region. There have been one or two alterations to the regions since 1948 but in essence the present London Midland Region covers the old LMS territory.

The LMS may have been the giant amongst railways but incredibly enough comparatively little is known about it. Every Great Western branch line may have been chronicled in great detail, and every Southern route written about but, apart from the locomotive histories, less is known about the LMS. There is no McDermot or Dendy Marshall for the LMS or even recent chronicles by K. Hoole or George Dow — the definitive history of the LMS has yet to be written.

The history of Britain's railways is one of cut-throat competition in the coal fields and speculative schemes to attract new passengers. The LNWR and the Midland fought one another before the grouping — and even after it!

The railways had it all their own way until the arrival of the "dreaded road motor", as one railway manager described it, and from then onwards it was a case of rationalisation and improvisation. The LNWR and L&YR pioneered the use of railmotors from as early as 1905 to fight tram and bus competition.

The LMS had the most amazing collection of minor railways, for some of the branch lines had started out at the dawn of the Railway Age. The Bolton & Leigh Railway, and the Cromford & High Peak were built by canal engineers and had steep inclines worked by cable. The Cromford & High Peak Railway functioned until 1967 under BR. The LMS owned the Burton & Ashby Light Railways, an electric tramway which was inherited from the Midland. The LMS owned the Wolverton & Stony Stratford steam tramway, a gem if ever there was. The LMS also had a large passenger terminal with a frequent service of trains which was never featured in a timetable or even shown on a map.

Closures of branch lines started during the twentieth century. Some railways ceased to function during the First World War, others during the 1930s, some lines were even bombed out during World War Two. Under London Midland Region management, many cross-country lines disappeared for ever during the 1950 to 1970 period. Few traditional rural branch lines exist today although a few LMS lines have been reopened as preserved railways. The LMS did not have much money to spend on the minor parts of the system, and many lines where they survived retained a distinctive pre-1923 flavour about them. Today, many disused railways have been converted to footpaths or cycle paths and some county councils even hire bicycles to be peddled over them in scenic areas. Some stations have been purchased and restored to their original condition, and it is still possible to see stations repainted in their original colours. LMS lines in Scotland have not been included as there is a separate book covering this subject entitled *Scottish Branch Lines 1955-1965*. Generally speaking, when a line loses its freight service, there is no other use for it — but there are, and have been, exceptions.

The SLS railtour near Rhymney on 5 January 1958 stops for photographers with the last train.

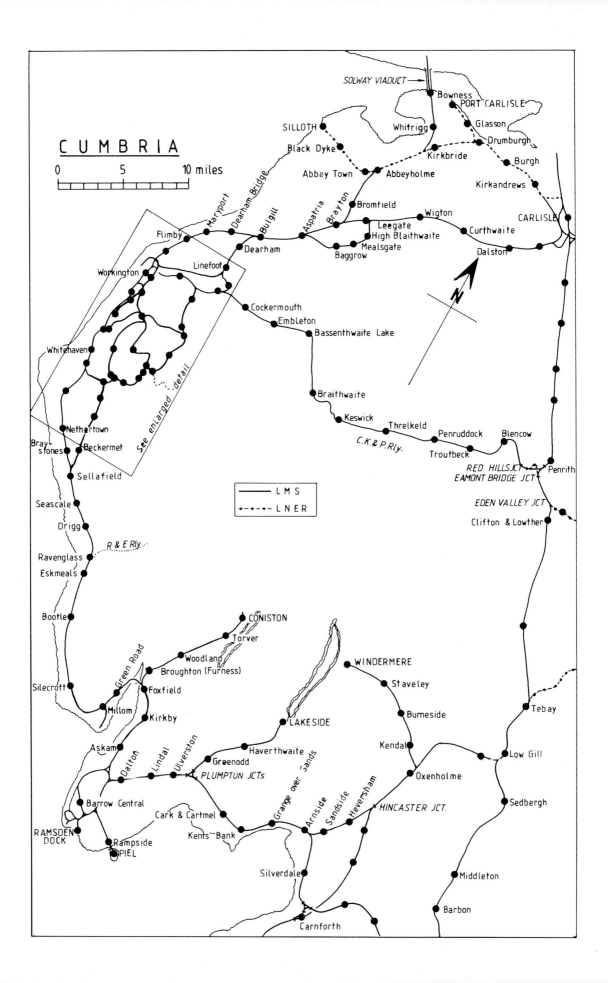

ULVERSTON TO LAKESIDE

The Furness Railway branch to Lakeside from Ulverston was 9¼ miles in length and connected with steamer services on Lake Windermere. The branch was opened to passengers on 1 June 1869, closed to regular passengers by the LMS on 26 September 1938 and used in the summer months by BR until 6 September 1965. Regular freight working ceased between Plumpton Jcn and Haverthwaite on 24 April 1967 but the line was visited by a railtour on 2 September 1967. The line was not lifted between Plumpton Jcn and Haverthwaite until May 1971, the section from Haverthwaite to Lakeside being reopened as the Lakeside & Haverthwaite Railway on 2 May 1973 by the Rt. Rev. Bishop of Wakefield, Eric Treacy.

Greenodd station has been demolished and the road now occupies the railway site for 2¾ miles. The road is now the improved A590.

The Lakeside & Haverthwaite Railway operates in connection with the Sealink-owned steamers and is now an established preserved railway. The line is 3½ miles long and follows the course of the River Leven to Lake Windermere. The locomotive stock at the opening of the line was two Class 4, 2-6-4 tanks 2072 and 2085, a "black five" 4-6-0 No 44806 (since removed), a Hunslet 0-6-0ST of 1953, a Bagnall 0-6-0ST of 1942, two Hudswell Clarke 0-6-0STs and a Peckett 0-4-0ST of 1937. In addition to the industrial steam locomotives, the line was endowed with a Fowler diesel, 0-4-0 "Fluff", a BR 0-6-0, diesel mechanical and an 0-4-0 petrol-driven machine called "Rachel" of 40 horse power built in 1924.

The railway has a good selection of rolling stock, the mainstay of the line being ex-BR Mk1 vehicles dating from 1951–1953. There is an intermediate halt at Newby Bridge which has been well restored, having been closed originally by the LMS in 1939. The railway runs a daily service from June to September.

The Lakeside & Haverthwaite has been a successful private railway serving a popular tourist area, the only controversial aspect having been the appearance of the locomotives. No 2085 was painted in Caledonian blue and No 2073 in LNWR black. Both liveries were, of course, never carried, as the locomotives were built at Brighton in 1950 and 1951. They were of a design by Fairburn for the LMS but were built by BR after 1948 and carried BR numbers.

OXENHOLME TO WINDERMERE

The 10-mile line from Oxenholme to Windermere, with through trains from Lancaster and Manchester in the summer, is still in being although the terminus at Windermere has been reduced in size. The line was considered to be the end of a main line in LMS days with through services to Euston. A named train, "The Lakes Express", even served the branch in BR days. The station has been converted into a supermarket at Windermere but with room for trains.

The line was authorised as the Kendal & Windermere Railway in 1845 and worked by the Lancaster & Carlisle Railway who opened from Lancaster to Kendal in 22 September 1846. Kendal to Windermere opened on 21 April 1847 and the Lancaster & Carlisle, which was useful to the LNWR, passed into LNWR ownership in 1879. The Windermere branch with intermediate stations at Kendal, Burnside and Staveley, was the first branch line in the Lake District.

HINCASTER JCN TO ARNSIDE

This section of line, operated by the Furness Railway, connected the Furness main coastal line with the West Coast Main Line at Hincaster Jcn, between Milnthorpe and Oxenholme. The 1922 passenger service was five trains per day from Grange-over-Sands to Kendal. Freight was more important and included coal, iron ore, and steel. The line opened on 26 June 1876.

The LMS withdrew regular passenger trains on 4 May 1942 temporarily, and the London Midland Region made the local passenger service withdrawal permanent from 1 March 1953. The LMS never admitted to permanent withdrawals on many of its lines, putting up "Service Suspended" notices and not reintroducing them. On the formation of BR in 1948, official closure dates were announced. The Arnside to Hincaster Jcn line had excursions, summer Saturday trains, and railtours until complete closure from 9 September 1963 of the through route. Sandside to Arnside lasted until 1 January 1972 for freight traffic.

PENRITH TO WORKINGTON

The Cockermouth, Keswick & Penrith Railway never had any rolling stock of its own and was worked by LNWR trains. The distance from Penrith to Cockermouth was 30¾ miles and the line opened on 2 January 1865. The railway passed through the heart of the Lake District with its fine mountain scenery.

The section from Cockermouth to Workington was built by the LNWR and was double track. In 1955 BR introduced diesel multiple unit trains over the line, this being one of the first lines in Britain to be supplied with two car "Derby lightweight" units. The West Cumberland area had iron ore and steelworks, and as a result of this the North Eastern Railway worked through coke trains from the Stainmore line via Eden Valley Jcn and Red Hills Jcn. BR closed the line to all traffic, on 6 March 1972 from Penrith to Keswick, and 18 April 1966 from Keswick to Workington. The section from Penrith to Blencon Quarry remained in use until 19 June 1972.

Travellers today can drive over a section of the railway as the line between Braithwaite and Cockermouth to Marron Jcn is now the new A66, one of the longest rail-to-road conversions in Britain so far. Bassenthwaite Lake is alongside the A66. There is a railway museum at Keswick situated on the first floor of 28 Main Street, Keswick. The exhibition is of local railway history with a model railway and shop. The Keswick Railway Museum is open daily from March to October from 2.00pm to 5.00pm. The Keswick to Troutbeck trackbed is to be turned into a footpath.

FOXFIELD TO CONISTON

The Furness Railway opened the 9½ mile branch from Foxfield to Coniston on 18 June 1859 to passengers. There was a growing tourist trade in the district and copper mines at Coniston. The Coniston Railway was incorporated into the Furness Railway in 1862. The extension to the copper mines beyond Coniston was opened in 1860.

The station building at Coniston was of a distinctive architectural style in keeping with the scenic grandeur of the district. The station was built in "Swiss Cottage" style with an overall roof and two island platforms, the two inner faces being under the enclosed roof area. The Furness Railway operated motor trains from 1905 which became "push and pull" under the LMS and BR. Motive power during pre-war years was LNWR or L&YR 2-4-2Ts, an example of which has been preserved. During BR days, Ivatt 2-6-2Ts worked the line and continued until the branch was closed to passengers on 6 October 1958. Freight was withdrawn on 30 April 1962.

The unique station buildings at Coniston have been demolished, and from Torver towards Broughton the A593 road covers the course of the line for half a mile. Torver, and Woodland stations are now private houses and Torver to Coniston station site is now a 2¼ mile long footpath. An excellent booklet entitled *The Coniston Railway*, depicting a Furness Railway train in Coniston station, is in sale locally and published by the Cumbrian Railways Association.

BARROW CENTRAL TO PIEL

Piel to Dalton was opened in 1846 and was the first section of the Furness Railway. The first locomotives and rolling stock were delivered to the Furness Railway by sea at Piel for the opening to Kirkby, which was on 12 August 1846. On opening, a direct steamer service was run from Fleetwood, the coastal section of the Furness via Ulverston to Carnforth not being opened until 1857. After completion of the Furness main line over the Leven and Kent estuaries, the Piel branch lost its importance, the service being withdrawn on 6 July 1936 by the LMS. A portion of the trackbed from Roosecote to Rampside, a distance of 2½ miles, is now a footpath. Piel Pier is now lost in a British Gas development on Piel Island.

Barrow Shipyard also had an unadvertised workmen's service which was withdrawn on 3 July 1967.

WEST CUMBERLAND

The discovery of iron ore in West Cumberland brought about industrialisation in the district, and in the mid nineteenth century railway companies were scrambling for the lucrative ore and coal traffic. All of the large companies competed with one another and even the North Eastern became involved with coke trains from County Durham to the steelworks on the West coast.

The first railway on the scene was the Maryport & Carlisle; which was opened by 1845. A loop from Aikbank Jcn to Aspatria via Mealsgate was completed on 1 October 1878. The M&CR also had a branch from Bullgill to Brigham known as the Derwent branch, a distance of 6¼ miles. This line was opened on 1 June 1867. The M&CR worked a passenger service from Maryport to Cockermouth and also from Carlisle via this route over which passenger trains ran until 27 April 1935. Freight services were discontinued shortly afterwards, there being little use for the line after the 1923 amalgamation and closure of the Solway Junction Railway. On the Mealsgate loop, Aikbank Jcn to Mealsgate closed to all traffic on 1 August 1921. Passenger trains were withdrawn from Mealsgate to Aspatria on 22 September 1930 and freight on 1 December 1952.

The Caledonian Railway invaded the area by way of the Solway Junction Railway, built to convey iron ore to the steelworks of Lanarkshire. The SJR left the Caledonian Railway at Kirtlebridge on the main line, crossed the Solway Firth on a mile long viaduct, ran over the North British Silloth branch to Abbeytown Jcn and connected with the M&CR at Brayton. The SJR was opened on 13 September 1869 and closed to all traffic on 1 September 1921, the viaduct being unsafe. The LMS demolished the viaduct in 1935 and lifted the CR track back to Brayton Jcn soon afterwards. The Solway Viaduct was used by Scottish pedestrians on Sundays, enabling them to drink in England. Abbeyholme Jcn to Brayton closed to all traffic on 1 September 1921 with the viaduct route, but reopened in May 1922 and was used until 14 February 1933 for freight and excursions.

The Whitehaven Cleator & Egremont Railway opened in 1866 from Whitehaven (Mirehouse Jcn) to Moor Row and Marron Jcn via Rowrah. The railway was built chiefly to convey iron ore and limestone, but passengers were conveyed from the outset. The railway became jointly owned by the LNWR and Furness from 1878. The LNWR ran the passenger trains as on the Workington–Penrith line. The FR ran the goods services south of Rowrah and the the LNWR north thereof. Passenger services were withdrawn by the LMS from Moor Row to Camerton on 13 April 1931 and freight by BR to Marron Jcn from Rowrah on 18 November 1960. Moor Row to Rowrah Hall Quarry and Arlecdon was closed by BR to all traffic from 1 April 1978. The WC&ER opened a branch from Ullock to Distington and Parton to serve new blast furnaces at Distington and was completed by 1 June 1881. This mineral-only line was used to convey iron ore and limestone into Distington and iron out to the coast, but closed in 1922. The passenger service from Sellafield to Whitehaven via Beckermet was withdrawn on 16 June 1947, with

Beckermet to Sellafield closing completely on 19 January 1970. The WC&ER opened this route in 1868. Sellafield to Egremont school trains ran until 3 March 1969. Beckermet Mines to Corkickle (via Moor Row) closed to all traffic on 6 October 1980 and the track has recently been lifted.

The Cleator & Workington Junction Railway was incorporated in 1876 and financed locally, as the owners of the steelworks and collieries felt that the LNWR and FR were charging too much for conveying ore, coal, and steel products. The C&WJR was set up to oppose the existing companies and ran from Moor Row (Cleator Jcn) to Siddick, Linefoot Jcn, and Rowrah. The system was started in 1879 and completed by 1887. The C&WJR owned its own locomotives but did not have any passenger vehicles, these being supplied by the FR. The railway was independent until the 1923 grouping, when absorbed into the LMS. A passenger service was run but was fairly sparse, the Calva Jcn to Linefoot section and Oatlands closing in 1922. The Lowca to Workington Central passenger service ceased on 31 May 1926, and the Moor Row to Siddick service on 13 April 1931. By the early thirties the iron had run out and many of the iron and steel works had closed, with resulting unemployment and a decline on both passenger and freight lines. Moor Row to Distington closed to freight on 16 September 1963 and the "main line" through to Calva Jcn by 15 June 1964. The Distington to Arlecdon line closed to freight in 1938. The only open section of the system at present is the Siddick and Calva Jcn, to Broughton Moor line. The railway to Broughton Moor runs to a Ministry of Defence depot, the traffic being very spasmodic. Workington Central is now a car park, and footpaths run from Workington Central to Calva Jcn, Lowca, and Moresby Parks.

Cockermouth, with lightweight multiple unit vehicles about to start for Workington, West Cumberland, on 31 July 1962. This was one of the first routes on BR to be dieselised with such units in 1955. The Keswick to Workington line closed to all traffic on 18 April 1966. The CK&PR was worked by LNWR trains, the CK&PR not possessing its own passenger stock. The section from Braithwaite to Cockermouth is now the main A66 road. Photograph by R. Joanes.

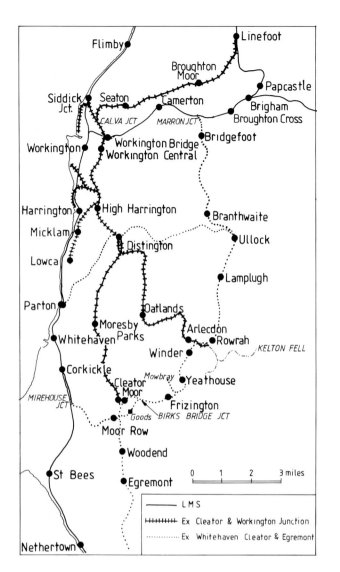

The railways' scramble for the coal and iron ore traffic in West Cumbria is illustrated by the map of the area. The Furness Railway with the London & North Western acquired the Whitehaven Cleator & Egremont in 1878. The Cleator & Workington Junction Railway was financed by local business interests to break the hold that the Furness and LNWR had acquired on mineral traffic. The C&WJR was complete by 1887 and made a connection with the Caledonian Railway via Linefoot Junction. Both systems became part of the LMS in 1923 and when the iron ore ran out in the 1930s much of the C&WJR was closed.

The only section in use today apart from the "main line" from Carlisle to Sellafield via Workington, is the Broughton Moor branch. Broughton Moor on the former C&WJR receives trains very rarely from Siddick Jct by way of Calva Jcn. The Rowrah & Kelton Fell Mineral Railway joined the WC&E Joint at Kelton Fell Junction near Rowrah. The line was 3½ miles long, was opened in 1877 and was built to convey the limestone used in the West Cumberland steelworks. This standard gauge mineral line closed in 1927.

L. & N. W. RY.
Cleator Moor

"The Lakes Express" arrives at Bassenthwaite Lake behind class 2 2-6-0 No 78018 on 30 July 1962 — photograph by R. Joanes.

Calva Junction, in the upper picture, shows Furness Railway D5 class (BR 52501) 0-6-0 built by Kitson in 1918 with an SLS/MLS special in 1954. Photo by C.H.A. Townley. The lower picture shows the CK&PR in steam days with "Cauliflowers" crossing at Cockermouth.

Staveley station on the Windermere branch with a Sunday ballast train worked by 8F 2-8-0 No 48600 on 22 August 1965 in the upper picture and the Solway Viaduct in the lower. The photograph below shows the viaduct before demolition which took place between 1933 and 1935. Scotsmen used to walk across the viaduct on Sundays for a drink. Photo by Loco & Gen. Rly. Photos.

reenodd, on the former Lakeside branch, with class 4, 2-6-4T No 42136 arriving on 2 August 1962. Photograph by R. Joanes. The lower
otograph shows Coniston in early BR days with a class 2, 2-6-2T blowing off steam under the overall roof. Photo by Lens of Sutton. Note
e LMS noticeboard in the background.

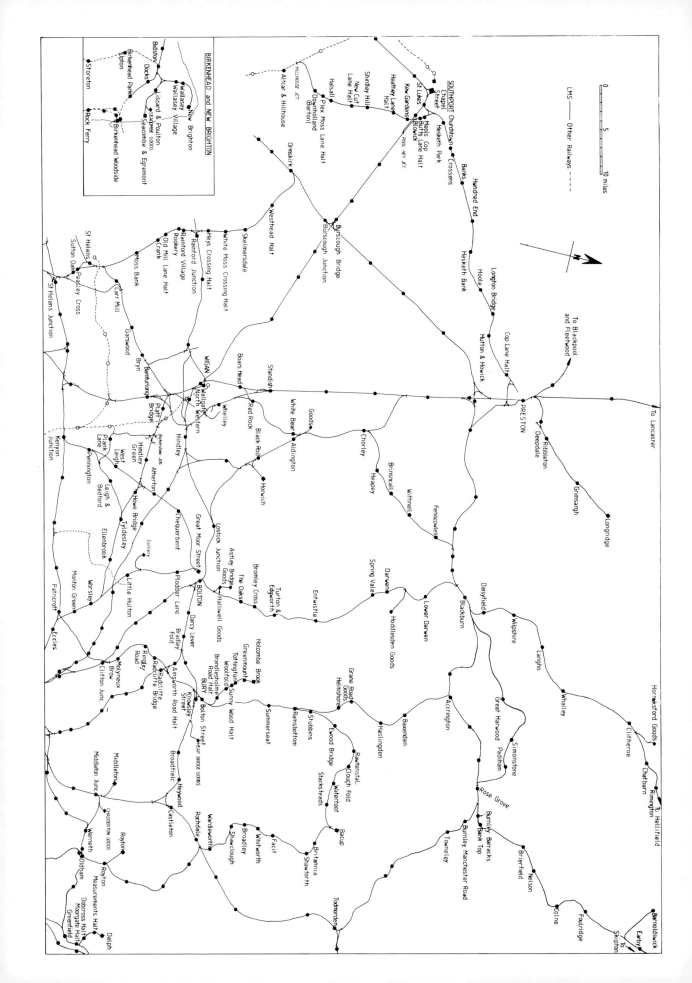

ROCHDALE TO BACUP

The 9 mile line from Rochdale to Bacup was completed throughout on 1 December 1881 and terminated at the existing Bacup station of the former East Lancashire Railway from Bury. The branch traversed the highest point on the former Lancashire & Yorkshire Railway and had some severe gradients. Eleven trains per day ran each way, on weekdays only, at the Grouping, but the LMS withdrew passenger services in 1947. The last passenger train ran on 16 June 1947 behind a class 3, 2-6-2T and two coaches. The Bacup to Facit section closed to goods on 5 May 1952 and Facit to Whitworth on 12 August 1963. The remaining section from Whitworth to Rochdale was closed to freight on 21 August 1967. The Whitworth to Rochdale section was traversed by a railtour organised by the Locomotive Club of Great Britain on 19 February 1967 when L&YR "pug" No 51218 did three trips over the line with brakevans. In its heyday the line conveyed heavy goods traffic including stone, cotton and coal. The line was single track between Wardleworth and Facit.

Today, part of the line can be walked as a mile of trackbed including the Healey Dell viaduct has been converted for the use of walkers through the Healey Dell Nature Reserve. This was opened by the local authority in 1972 and is used by naturalists and local walkers. Whitworth to Facit is now a road and the station entrance to Shawforth now forms an entry into a housing estate.

BACUP TO STUBBINS JCN

The East Lancashire Railway from Manchester opened Stubbins Jcn to Rawtenstall on 25 September 1846 and was extended to Bacup on 1 October 1852. In its heyday the line conveyed considerable goods traffic in the form of raw cotton, coal and wool to the various private sidings and mills. There was a sizeable loco shed at Bacup with four roads. Looking at old photographs of the line in L&YR days, with heavy freight trains and sidings crammed with wagons loaded for export, it seems incredible that the line was closed for all traffic by BR on 5 December 1966 between Rawtenstall and Bacup. In pre-Grouping days, traffic was so heavy on the line that goods trains had to be run at night as well as during the daytime. Even during BR days a passenger service every ½ hour ran, doubling to every 15 minutes on Saturdays (per 1962 timetable) to Bacup.

The section from Rawtenstall to Bury (Bolton St) was closed to passengers by BR from 5 June 1972. The track from Rawtenstall to Bury is still in position and under restoration by the East Lancs Railway, the goods traffic having been withdrawn in December 1980.

Bacup station site today is now occupied by a factory. The station was unusual in that it served as the terminus for two branch lines heading off in different directions. The goods warehouse near Stacksteads can still be seen and has been converted into offices. The two single tunnels at Thrutch can be observed as can the pub at Waterfoot known as "The Railway". The section of line from Clough Fold Gasworks to Rawtenstall is now the new main road.

THE EAST LANCS RAILWAY

A newly operational railway run by preservationists is the East Lancs Railway (Bury) which was opened for passengers on 25 July 1987. The service runs from the Bolton St station terminus of the ELR to Ramsbottom, a distance of 4 miles. The ELR are hoping to extend to Irwell Vale in 1988, and on to Rawtenstall in 1989 (another 4 miles). The railway is being assisted by grants from local government and the Manpower Services Commission. The East Lancashire Railway Preservation Society are well situated in Bury with their Bolton St terminus which was extensively rebuilt and modernised by BR, following a fire. The East Lancs have a museum situated in the large goods shed at Castlecroft Road, housing a varied selection of locomotives and rolling stock. Opening took place with the ex Manchester Ship Canal loco No 32 (HC of 1903), an 0-6-0T named "Gothenburg" and Meaford Power Station No 1 (RSH). The ELR already have class 9F 92207, class 4MT 80097, BR class 5 73156, LMS class 5 45337 and a good selection of diesels including D832, D7076, D1041, 40.145, D5054 (24.054), although most of these need some attention — the steam locos especially.

BURY (BOLTON ST) TO HOLCOMBE BROOK

This 3¼ mile branch commenced from Bolton Street station and had seven intermediate halts, being opened by the L&YR on 6 November 1882. The initial train service was of six trains each way daily serving three intermediate points at Woolfold, Tottington, and Greenmount. In July 1905, the L&YR introduced a steam railmotor service and opened additional rail level halts at Woodhall Road, Brandleshome Road, Sunny Wood, and Knowles Level Crossing. The railmotor service was operated in response to the tramway competition which was taking a lot of patronage from the branch. The line was electrified on 29 July 1913 on a 3,500 volt dc overhead system, the equipment being supplied by Dick Kerr & Co on an experimental basis. A unique locomotive was used to operate the line which had a steeple cab, bow collectors, and was mounted on a standard Aspinall 2-4-2T frame.

The branch ran on the dc system until 29 March 1918 when it was converted to the L&YR 1200 dc protected third rail system. Two of the halts were closed in 1918 with the new electrification. The 1200 volt dc system lasted until 24 March 1951, by which time the equipment was deemed to be worn out. BR re-introduced steam working in 1951 using the traditional

L&YR 2-4-2Ts and railmotor units. The passenger service lasted until 5 May 1952 and freight trains until 2 May 1960 when the line was cut back to Tottington Sidings. The final piece of line lasted until 19 August 1963 when the Bury to Tottington freight only section was closed. Holcombe Brook today has been built upon and the site is now occupied by houses and a supermarket. The parts of the line that have not been built upon can still be walked over.

RAMSBOTTOM TO ACCRINGTON
The East Lancs Railway presently terminates at Ramsbottom and will extend to Rawtenstall on the former Bacup branch. Accrington to Stubbins Jcn was opened by the original East Lancs Railway on 17 August 1848 and closed by BR on 5 December 1966 to all traffic — the same day as Bacup to Rawtenstall. The line was a through route and was used by Manchester to Colne trains, which now run from Colne to Preston. The intermediate stations were at Helmshore, Haslingden and Baxenden. Helmshore station is now a private house where the L&YR signalbox and goods shed survive. At Haslingden the A56 by-pass road is built over the railway, obliterating Haslingden station, and Haslingden tunnel has been removed. Baxenden is demolished but there is a footpath thence to Accrington — a distance of 2¼ miles.

BLACKBURN TO BURNLEY VIA PADIHAM
The North Lancs Loop was opened to passengers from Rose Grove to Padiham on 1 September 1876, and extended to Blackburn on 15 October 1877. The distance from Blackburn to Rose Grove was 10 miles and the loop line proved to be a very useful alternative route, especially for Summer Saturdays and Sunday engineering works diversions. The regular passenger service was withdrawn on 2 December 1957 but the line was used on occasions until 1963 by passenger trains. The regular freight service was withdrawn on 2 November 1964 from Blackburn to Padiham. The Padiham to Rose Grove section is still retained to supply oil to Padiham power station but the stations on the line have disappeared. Several parts of the trackbed have either been converted into a footpath, or are planned for conversion.

DELPH TO OLDHAM (THE DELPH DONKEY)
The picturesque village of Delph, popular with day trippers and within easy reach of Manchester, was served by a short 2-mile branch line with through trains from Oldham via the LNW main line at Greenfield. The line opened from Greenfield on 1 September 1851 with a meagre service but in 1910 the LNWR put on a railmotor service. The LNWR opened two new halts at Moorgate and Dobcross in 1912 and the LMS opened a halt at Measurements in 1932 — this was named after a nearby mill. Under BR the push & pull service lasted until 2 May 1955, when the service to passengers was withdrawn between Oldham Clegg Street and Delph via Greenfield. The line was railtoured after closure by a special train organised by the SLS/MLS. Freight services lasted until 4 November 1963 on the Delph branch and 13 April 1964 on the Greenfield to Oldham section. The "main line" from Diggle via Upper Mill was taken out of use after 30 November 1966.

Visitors to Delph today can easily be fooled into thinking that the line is still open, for Delph station still exists and has track with rolling stock on it. In 1970 a coach was installed on a length of track as an annexe to the station building and used by a physiotherapist. The station yard is used by Huddersfield Plant Hire and the short length of track houses a brakevan and an oiltank wagon. (For a period during the 1970s an industrial steam loco, an 0-6-0ST, was also kept on this section of track.)

GREATER MANCHESTER
Passenger services over the Bury Bolton St to Castleton North and South section and the Rochdale—Bury—Bolton line ceased on 5 October 1970, the section from Bury to Bolton East Jcn closing to all traffic. Rawtenstall coal depot closed at the end of 1980 (the goods depot is now a car showroom) and the line is disused as far as Heywood. Most of the line, the section from Bury Bolton St to Rawtenstall will become part of the new East Lancs Railway. Plans are afoot, put forward by the local authority, to convert the disused sections to footpaths. The Heap Bridge goods-only branch closed in December 1973. Yates, Duxbury's mill, at Heap Bridge, was shunted by steam locos until the time the line closed. In the same area, Clifton Jcn to Radcliffe North Jcn closed to all traffic on 5 December 1966, and Radcliffe North Jcn to Bradley Fold Jcn closed completely on 2 November 1964. Some sections of these lines are scheduled to be converted to footpaths or cycle paths. Patricroft to Clifton Jcn closed to all traffic on 28 April 1953 with the collapse of Clifton tunnel. From then on, the southern end of the line was used for wagon storage until 1959.

Of the goods-only lines in the area, Astley Bridge ceased to function on 4 September 1961 and Halliwell to Bolton on 3 August 1981. The L&YR 1-mile long branch to Manchester Docks, Salford, closed on 15 June 1964. BR still use most of the Horwich branch, which had a passenger service until 27 September 1965, as access to the works. The site of Horwich station is grassed over. The 1-mile long Middleton to Middleton Jcn branch, with through trains to Manchester, closed to passengers on 7 September 1964 and freight on 11 October 1965. The station site is now occupied by the Crown Wallpaper distribution depot but part of the route is still walkable. The 1¼ mile Royton branch closed to all traffic on 18 April 1966 — a public footpath extends over the line to the former junction. Royton station site has now been built upon but "The Railway Hotel" commemorates the former Lancashire & Yorkshire Railway terminus. The Rochdale to Oldham line was opened for passengers on 2 November 1863 with the Royton branch opening on 21 March 1864. The recently closed Royton station was the former Royton Jcn. Chadderton Jcn to Oldham Werneth closed to all traffic on 7 January 1963, though Chadderton Coal Depot remains open.

BOLTON (GREAT MOOR ST) & BRANCHES

The Bolton & Leigh Railway, one of the earliest of railways, was engineered by George Stephenson and opened on 1 August 1828, thus preceding the Liverpool & Manchester by nearly two years. The railway was built to provide a link between Bolton and the Leeds & Liverpool canal. The railway was engineered on canal lines, with cable-worked inclines instead of locks, similar to the Cromford & High Peak. The cable-worked inclines were abolished in 1885 when the LNWR built a new line to replace them.

The Bolton & Leigh Railway was joined to the Liverpool and Manchester main line by the Kenyon & Leigh Jcn Railway on 1 January 1831. All became part of the LNWR after 1846 and Great Moor St station was rebuilt in 1874. Passenger services over the Bolton to Kenyon Jcn line were terminated by BR on 29 March 1954 but freight traffic lasted until the 1960s. The freight traffic wound down slowly and the line closed in sections from 1963 to 1969, the last section from Pennington to Kenyon closing to all traffic on 5 May 1969. Most of the line at the northern end has been built upon, but Howe Bridge to Pennington has been converted into a road and forms the new A580 Leigh by-pass. The Pennington to Kenyon section is now a footpath.

The LNWR "main line" from Manchester to Bolton Great Moor St via Worsley and Little Hulton was opened from Worsley (Roe Green Jcn) to Bolton on 1 April 1875, competing with the L&YR for the Bolton to Manchester traffic. After the 1922 amalgamation the two routes became duplicated, but it was not until 29 March 1954 that BR withdrew the passenger service. Freight trains were withdrawn between Roe Green Jcn (Worsley) and Little Hulton Jcn from 20 October 1960. With the closure of Little Hulton Colliery, the line was cut back to Plodder Lane on 11 May 1964. The line was finally cut back from Plodder Lane to Bolton (GMS) on 1 July 1965 and closed to all traffic. Little Hulton to Worsley is now a footpath.

Some main line trains ran from Manchester to Liverpool via Tyldesley and Kenyon Jcn, the route being a useful alternative for engineering diversions. The LNWR opened the line from Eccles to Wigan and Tyldesley to Pennington on 1 September 1864. This prevented the rival L&YR from building a more direct Liverpool & Manchester line. The L&YR had difficulties in competing with the LNWR for the Liverpool to Manchester traffic because of the longer route via Wigan. Tyldesley to Wigan, being part of the LNWR main line, had some fast train services but, as this was yet another duplicate route, BR closed it to passengers on 2 November 1964. The passenger service had been reduced to only three trains per day by closure. Eccles, Tyldesley and Kenyon Jcn finally closed to all traffic from 5 May 1969 but most of the route all the way round from Monton Green to Kenyon Jcn has been converted by Greater Manchester Council into a footpath as well as the Tyldesley to Howe Bridge section. Tyldesley to Chequerbent was closed to goods on 6 January 1969 and Howe Bridge through to Bickershaw Jcn on 11 February 1975. Pennington to Bickershaw ceased operations on 13 September 1965.

BROADHEATH TO DITTON JCN

Broadheath (Skelton Jcn) to Warrington still exists as a double-track railway but there are presently no trains between Skelton West Jcn and Arpley Jcn. The Engineer has stopped trains as the railway bridge over the Manchester Ship Canal at Latchford is unsafe. The section of line from Warrington to Broadheath was opened on 1 May 1854 as the Warrington & Altrincham Junction Railway and was purchased by the LNWR in 1864. The bridge over the Manchester Ship Canal was opened when the canal was completed in 1894, involving a realignment of the line at the MSC's cost.

The St Helens Railway, or The St Helens Canal & Railway to give it its full title, extended from Widnes to Warrington on 1 February 1853 and was connected to the Warrington to Broadheath line for the opening on 1 May 1854. Passenger services from Ditton Jcn to Broadheath were withdrawn by BR on 10 September 1962, the service being Ditton Jcn to Manchester. In Pre-Grouping days the LNWR ran a through service via this route from Liverpool to Manchester. The distance from Ditton Jcn to Broadheath is 18¼ miles.

Today the section from Warrington to Ditton Jcn is used by freight trains for chemical, stone, cement and coal traffic, which have been diverted following the closure of the Warrington to Broadheath section. The stations have been demolished but some station houses and signalboxes still exist. The station house and signalbox at Dunham Massey survive and at Heatley & Warburton the station buildings are still in existence. Local opinion is that there have been no trains for two years (1987). The official date of closure by BR was given as 6 May 1985.

ST HELENS TO WIDNES

The St Helens & Runcorn Gap Railway opened on 21 February 1833, providing an outlet for the collieries in the area to the docks on the Mersey at Widnes. The railway was essentially a coal-carrying line but a passenger service was provided from St Helens (Shaw St) to Ditton Jcn as well as a shuttle from St Helens Jcn to St Helens (Shaw St). The passenger service from

St Helens (Shaw St) to Ditton Jcn was withdrawn on 18 June 1951. St Helens Shaw St was renamed Central from 5 October 1987. St Helens to St Helens Jcn closed to passengers on 14 June 1965. The line south of Sutton Manor Colliery to Widnes closed to all traffic on 6 August 1981. Sutton Manor to Sutton Oak Jcn is disused and the stations and halts have been demolished, but the track is still in position. Sutton Manor Colliery to Sutton Oak Jcn was officially closed from 5 Oct 1987.

RAINFORD JCN TO ST HELENS AND ORMSKIRK
St Helens to Rainford Jcn opened on 1 February 1858 and made a connection with the L&YR main line from Liverpool to Wigan. The extension on to Ormskirk was opened by the ELR on 1 March 1858. The countryside changes from St Helens to Ormskirk, the industrial scenery giving way to flat agricultural land. The route was the haunt of steam railmotors introduced in 1906, when new halts were introduced between Ormskirk and Rainford Jcn serving rural areas. Ormskirk is the terminus of the line from Liverpool, originally electrified by the L&YR in 1913. The former Liverpool–Ormskirk–Preston main line, on which through expresses once operated, has now been reduced in status, the section from Ormskirk to Preston being operated as a single track branch utilising DMMU stock. A similar operation exists between Kirkby and Rainford where a through service to Manchester is provided. There is no through service from Liverpool to Manchester via the former L&YR route today. On the former St Helens to Rainford–Ormskirk branches freight traffic ceased from Ormskirk to Skelmersdale on 18th November 1963 and back to Rainford by 16 September 1961. On the St Helens to Rainford section, the St Helens to Old Mill Lane part closed on 30 January 1967 and on to Rainford on 6 July 1964, to all traffic. There is not much to see today. The trackbed from Rainford Village back to St Helens is now a footpath known as Rainford Linear Park, and Skelmersdale new town has obliterated most of the railway. There is a road built on the course of the railway at Skelmersdale and another road named after the railway.

LIVERPOOL & MERSEYSIDE
The Liverpool & Manchester Railway opened up for business on 15 September 1830 at Liverpool Crown St for passengers and Wapping Dock for goods. When the docks extended northwards, more feeder lines were built by the major railway companies and Canada Dock to Edge Hill opened for goods on 15 October 1866. Passenger trains commenced to run on 1 July 1870. A branch to Alexandra Dock from the Canada Dock line opened to passengers on 1 September 1881. All these lines were part of the LNWR system, the LNWR having been formed after 1846 by amalgamations. The Lime St line was opened on 15 August 1836. The LNWR opened Edge Hill to Waterloo Dock on 1 August 1849. Both the Waterloo and Wapping lines were cable worked. A passenger station on the docks at Riverside was opened in 1895 and boat trains used this line over the Mersey Docks & Harbour Board lines via Waterloo and Edge Hill. Riverside was used by boat trains until 1 March 1971, with the branch from Edge Hill closing to goods by 8 April 1973. Wapping Dock (Park Lane Goods) closed to all traffic on 1 November 1965. The passenger service over the Edge Hill to Bootle (Canada Dock) branch ceased to Canada Dock from 5 May 1941 as a result of bombing but Alexandra Dock closed officially on 26 February 1949, although the service finished in 1948. The LMS as a rule did not admit to closures as such, usually suspending the service until further notice. Regular passenger trains did work over the Edge Hill to Bootle junction section until 8th May 1978 as the Lime Street to Southport through coaches direct from Euston came this way. The route is still in use to Seaforth freightliner depot. The Midland Railway branch from Fazakerley Jcn to Langton Dock closed on 1 January 1968 to all traffic. Canada Dock to Atlantic Jcn closed to all traffic on 3 September 1982.

The Wirral Railway, formerly the Seacombe, Hoylake & Deeside Railway, opened to New Brighton on 30 March 1888 with the Seacombe branch following on 1 June 1895. The LMS electrified to New Brighton on 14 March 1938 and a through service to Liverpool continues under BR. Passengers to Seacombe were not so lucky as the branch closed to passengers on 4 January 1960 with freight following on 17 June 1963. The trackbed was utilised to form the approach to the new Mersey road tunnel in 1971.

SOUTHPORT TO DOWNHOLLAND (BARTON)
The line from Southport to Barton was opened on 1 September 1887 from Meols Cop and extended to Altcar & Hillhouse on 1 October 1887. The railway opened as the Liverpool, Southport & Preston Junction Railway but was worked by the West Lancashire Railway, which was in turn incorporated into the Lancashire & Yorkshire in 1897. The passenger service was from Southport to Barton, although the line made a connection with the Cheshire Lines at Altcar & Hillhouse (Hillhouse Jcn). The L&YR ran a railmotor service over the 8 miles from Southport to Barton, the service being 10 trains per day at grouping, four of which ran through to Altcar. Rail level halts were provided for the railmotors introduced in 1906. Barton was renamed Downholland in 1924 and passenger trains from there to Altcar were withdrawn on 15 November 1926. Downholland to Meols Cop (Southport) passenger services ceased on 26 September 1938. Freight services were withdrawn from Meols Cop to Altcar (Butts Lane Jcn–Hillhouse Jcn) on 21 January 1952, although Downholland to Altcar did not have a regular freight service. Shirdley Hill to Butts Lane Jcn was used for storage of empty stock until 1964. Shirdley Hill station site is now occupied by a small housing estate but a plaque in Shaws Garth commemorates the local railway and reads "Site of Shirdley Hill Railway Station on the Southport to Downholland Branch Line; closed to passengers 1938 — stationmaster Thomas Shaw." Another relic is Halsall post office which was the old station. The trackbed from Halsall to Hillhouse Jcn and beyond on the former Cheshire Lines is a nature reserve maintained by the local authority who issue permits to botanists who walk the old trackbed.

Seacombe, with N5 class No 69290 about to work the 2.29 pm to Wrexham Central on 14 August 1954. These locos were ex MSLR 0-6-2Ts, classified N5 by the LNER — photograph by Hugh Ballantyne.

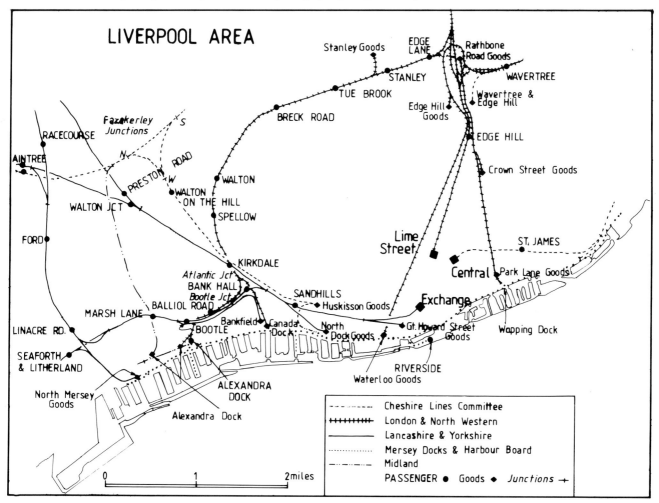

LIVERPOOL AREA

Stanley Goods
EDGE LANE
Rathbone Road Goods
STANLEY
WAVERTREE
TUE BROOK
Wavertree & Edge Hill
Edge Hill Goods
BRECK ROAD
EDGE HILL
Crown Street Goods
Fazakerley Junctions
RACECOURSE
PRESTON ROAD
WALTON
AINTREE
WALTON ON THE HILL
WALTON JCT
SPELLOW
Lime Street
ST. JAMES
FORD
KIRKDALE
Central
Park Lane Goods
Atlantic Jct
BANK HALL
Bootle Jct
SANDHILLS
BALLIOL ROAD
Huskisson Goods
Exchange
MARSH LANE
Bankfield
Canada Dock
North Dock Goods
Gt. Howard Street Goods
Wapping Dock
LINACRE RD.
BOOTLE
SEAFORTH & LITHERLAND
RIVERSIDE
Waterloo Goods
North Mersey Goods
ALEXANDRA DOCK
Alexandra Dock

- - - - - - Cheshire Lines Committee
+++++++ London & North Western
———— Lancashire & Yorkshire
.... Mersey Docks & Harbour Board
— - — Midland
PASSENGER ● Goods ◆ Junctions →

0   1   2miles

SOUTHPORT TO PRESTON

Opened throughout as the West Lancashire Railway on 16 September 1882, the line was taken over by the L&YR in 1897. The line ran through sparsely populated countryside, flat, and full of market gardens. The area was more akin to the Fens than Lancashire and as a consequence little remains to be seen of the line as most stations have been demolished. The branch is in fact one of the most obliterated in the country, only part of the station buildings (now a house) remains at Hutton & Howick which is actually in New Longton. The Southport to Preston line had a branch to Tarleton which opened in 1881 from Hesketh Bank. On this 1-mile branch the L&YR introduced a railmotor in 1912 which only lasted until 1 October 1913. Passenger services from Southport to Preston were withdrawn on 7 September 1964, the section from Hesketh Park to Preston being to all traffic. The section from Hesketh Park to Meols Cop lasted to freight until 27 November 1967. Crossends was the terminus of the electrified service from Liverpool originally introduced by the L&YR in 1904 and upon closure in 1964 was one of the few instances in Britain of an electrified line being closed. The trackbed from Tarleton to Hesketh Bank is now a footpath.

PRESTON TO LONGRIDGE

The Preston & Longridge Railway opened on 1 May 1840, the 6½ mile line operating from a terminus at Deepdale in Preston. The railway was horse-worked to start with and the opening train was preceded by a brass band. The line was built to convey stone from the quarries at Longridge, the rails being laid on stone block sleepers. The railway management proposed an extension from Longridge northwards, but in 1847 work began on a new line from Grimsargh to Clitheroe. This extension was never completed by earthworks can still be seen today. The railway management introduced steam traction in 1848 but the company was not taken over by a larger organisation until 1867, when the L&YR and LNWR companies bought it. The L&YR and LNWR owned the line jointly from then until 1922, when it became part of the LNWR system. The L&YR and LNWR had been wary of the Midland Railway's intentions of expansion in the area. Passenger services were withdrawn on 2 June 1930 under LMS auspices and freight on 6 November 1967 from Longridge back to Courtaulds Sidings. Courtaulds Sidings to Deepdale Jcn closed on 18 February 1980.

The former terminus of the original Preston & Longridge Railway survives at Deepdale, being used by BR for the coal concentration depot. The original Deepdale station building, with rail-level flagstone platform, survives at the first level crossing, and the stone platform of the first station at Ribbleton may also be seen. The station site at Grimsargh is commemorated by "Old Station Close" but the real relic of the branch is the Towneley Arms at Longridge. The Towneley Arms was originally owned by the railway and was incorporated into the structure of the station, where the canopy still projects outward from the pub wall. Little has changed apart from the removal of the track. Visitors to Longridge are advised to visit the County Kitchen Cafe opposite the Towneley Arms, where a fine selection of photographs of the line can be seen on the walls. At Grimsargh the Whittingham Asylum Railway (1889–1957) connected with a passenger service over the two mile private branch to Whittingham Asylum. The Whittingham Railway was free to passengers and had an interesting collection of motive power, including a Stroudley D1 class 0-4-2 tank purchased secondhand from the Southern Railway and built in 1886. The Grimsargh Footpath extends for a mile southwards from Grimsargh station site and will extend to Deepdale Jcn.

BOLTON & BLACKBURN TO HELLIFIELD

The Bolton, Blackburn, Clitheroe & West Yorkshire Railway opened for business on 12 June 1848 between Bolton & Blackburn. The railway was extended to Chatburn on 21 June 1850. The whole line became part of the L&YR from 1859 and was extended from Chatburn to meet the Midland main line at Hellifield on 1 June 1880. The distance from Bolton to Hellifield is 38 miles. The Bolton to Blackburn section is still open to ordinary passenger traffic and cannot be termed a branch line but BR treat it as one. There was a branch of 2¼ miles to Hoddlesden which was opened on 1 October 1876 and closed back to Shaws Siding on 30 October 1950. This branch, which was freight only, closed from Shaws Siding to Hoddlesden Jcn on 3 May 1962. Today, passenger services remain from Manchester to Blackburn but no regular passenger service exists beyond, these having been withdrawn on 10 September 1962. Hellifield to Blackburn does see the occasional passenger train in the form of excursions and engineers' works diversions. The occasional steam working to Carlisle or Appleby also uses this line, which is quite scenic. The engineering works are heavy with the most noticeable feature being the 48 span Whalley viaduct all in brick. Regular freight working runs to Horrocksford Cement Works above Clitheroe, but freight beyond there depends mainly on diversions off the Carnforth line.

The station house at Newsholme is still used and in a good state of repair, having been converted into a private house. Gisburn and Rimington have well restored station buildings. The owner of the station house at Rimington is of the opinion that "it's only Ribble Cement that keeps the line going". At Chatburn the station house and buildings survive in a good state of repair but at Clitheroe the old station buildings are now a DIY store. At Whalley and Wilpshire the station buildings survive, whilst at Langho only the platform edges remain. At Daisyfield the platforms survive as does a L&YR signalbox, but the line has been singled at this point. The future of the line is in the balance depending mainly on the outcome of the Settle & Carlisle saga and the cement traffic. The cement works at Horrocksford saw major new investment in 1985, including rail-loading facilities.

BLACKBURN TO CHORLEY & WIGAN

The Blackburn to Chorley and Adlington Jcn to Boars Head Jcn lines were opened on 1 December 1869 and were jointly owned between the L&YR and LNWR. Known as the Lancashire Union Joint, the two sections became part of the LNWR in 1922 and LMS in 1923. The route proved to be a useful outlet from Wigan to the North Lancs area and was used by diversions off the West Coast Main Line. Blackburn (Cherry Tree Jcn) to Chorley and on to Wigan via Red Rock closed to passengers on 4 January 1960. Chorley to Feniscowles closed to freight on 3 January 1966, and Feniscowles to Cherry Tree on 22 April 1968. The situation today is unusual for although the track has been lifted there are some interesting relics to be seen. At Feniscowles a house has been built on the site of the station. At Withnell the whole station survives and has been bought by an enthusiast who has laid out a garden railway all around the location. The next station down the line at Brinscall has been totally erased but Heapey is now a boarding kennels and cattery, the buildings having been greatly extended. The Adlington Jcn to Boars Head section was closed to all traffic from 31 December 1971 and is now a public footpath for most of the route.

THE WHELLEY LINES

The Boars Head to Whelley and Hindley section of the former LNWR Wigan avoiding line is being converted into a footpath by the local authority. Regular freight traffic from Standish Jcn to Bamfurlong via Whelley ceased on 2 October 1972. The line was used by diversions in 1973 and occasional engineers' trains until track removal in 1976. Springs Branch was one of the earliest of branch lines and was opened in 1838 to a colliery. Virtually all colliery branch lines in the Wigan area are now defunct and there are proposals by the local council to convert more abandoned colliery lines into footpaths.

FLEETWOOD TO POULTON

The (P&WJt) LNWR & LYR line to Fleetwood can hardly be considered a branch line in the true sense, as through services were run to other parts of Lancashire off of the line. The line today functions as a branch line, as passenger services were withdrawn from 1 June 1970. Fleetwood proper to Wyre Dock closed to all traffic on 18 April 1966, the former Wyre Dock station being renamed Fleetwood on the same day. The present line runs to the disused power station at Fleetwood but ICI still use the line to Burn Naze, and a new contract for vinyl by rail to Barry will assure the line's future for a while yet.

GASTANG TO KNOTT END

The 11½ mile railway from Garstang & Catterall on the West Coast Main Line to Knott End, opposite Fleetwood, was promoted by local landowners who wanted a railway to convey their produce. The railway opened on 14 December 1870 to Pilling, was single track and worked by one engine only. "Hebe" was an 0-4-2 saddle tank built by Black Hawthorn & Co. When the locomotive was stopped for repair the train service was withdrawn until the repairs had been carried out! When "Hebe" finally expired the line closed, not be reopen until 1875 when another engine was found. The 4½ mile extension to Knott End was completed from Pilling in July 1908. The line prospered before the coming of the motorbus and in 1920 a steam railmotor was hired from the LNWR. The steam railmotor ran the passenger service until the line closed on 31 March 1930 to passengers. The freight service was withdrawn from Knott End to Pilling on 13 November 1950, and Pilling to Garstang Town on 1 July 1963. The final section from Garstang Town to Garstang & Catterall closed to freight trains on 19 July 1965.

The Garstang & Knott End Railway was independent until the 1923 grouping, the LNWR having shown little interest in acquisition. Under the LMS the railway declined and with the introduction of buses in the 1920s there was little hope of maintaining the passenger service. Part of the trackbed at Knott End is now a footpath. Knott End station building, close to the ferry landing for Fleetwood, survives as the "Knott End Café". Today, the original G&KER conveniences at the side of the buildings continue to serve their appointed purpose.

WENNINGTON TO HEYSHAM & MORECAMBE

The Midland main line from Wennington to Lancaster is now disused, the trains running via Carnforth over the former Furness & Midland joint line. The Midland line from Lancaster (Green Ayre) to Wennington was opened on 17 November 1849 and extended to Clapham on 1 June 1850. The railway was opened as the North Western Railway (not to be confused with the LNWR) and was eventually purchased by the Midland in 1871. The Lancaster to Morecambe line was opened on 12 June 1848 by the "little" North Western Railway. BR closed the Morecambe, Lancaster–Wennington section on 3 January 1966 to passengers and 5 June 1967 to freight. The Midland Railway opened a new station at Morecambe (Promenade) in 1907, the LNWR having opened their own Morecambe (Euston Road) on 9 May 1886. The LNWR station at Euston Road was closed on 15 September 1958 under BR ownership, although used as an excursion platform in later years.

The Midland opened the Heysham branch on 11 July 1904. There, ships were met by boat trains as well as a local railmotor service between Heysham and Morecambe. The shipping service from Heysham was Midland steamers to Belfast to link up with the newly acquired (1903) Belfast & Northern Counties Railway in Ireland. The Midland electrified the Heysham Harbour branch in 1908 concurrently with electrification to Lancaster Green Ayre and Castle. The London Midland Region discontinued and mostly abandoned the electrified system in 1966. Passenger boat trains continued to run on the Heysham line until 8 October 1975 when the Belfast Sealink service was discontinued. Today, from Caton on the old Midland main line to Green Ayre, there is a footpath which extends to Morecambe with the exception of the part over Greyhound Bridge — now part of the A589 road. A passenger service was re-introduced from Heysham on 11 May 1987 but was very half-hearted, consisting of one train per day connecting with the Isle of Man day boat. The train runs non-stop to Preston.

LANCASTER CASTLE TO GLASSON DOCK

The dock at Glasson was opened in 1787 and was connected to the Lancaster Canal in 1826. The owners opposed a rail connection, after the L&C main line had been built through Lancaster in the 1840s. The branch opened to passengers on 9 July 1883 and closed on 7 July 1930. The timetable at the grouping in 1923 included eight trains per weekday. The line was 5 miles long and included an intermediate halt at Conder Green, 4 miles from Lancaster. The line was visited by an SLS/MLS railtour on Sunday 29 May 1960 — probably the last passenger train to traverse it. Most of the trackbed is now a walk known as "The Lune Estuary Coastal Path". BR closed the line to freight traffic on 7 September 1964.

Heysham Harbour in April 1952 with 0-4-4T No 41904. The passesnger service was withdrawn on 8 October 1975 but reinstated on 11 May 1987.

Knott End terminus of the former Garstang & Knott End Railway as seen in 1955. Passenger services were withdrawn on 31 March 1930 by the LMS but freight lasted until 13 November 1950. The building is now the "Knott End Cafe". Photographs by C.H.A. Townley.

The weeds have taken over at Glasson Dock in this May 1960 photograph showing the LNWR wooden station building in the background.

Fleetwood (above), with DMMU unit and single platform. Fleetwood as it was, now demolished (below). The rails have been removed in this 1968 photograph. Both photographs by R. Joanes, taken on 14 December 1968.

The changing scene at Longridge, in the above photograph ex LNWR 0-8-0 No 49451 hauls the RCTS Mid Lancs Railtour on Saturday 22 September 1962. In the picture below of the same location today, the Towneley Arms Hotel has remained unscathed, even the canopy of the station platform remains in place. The Hotel was once owned by the railway.

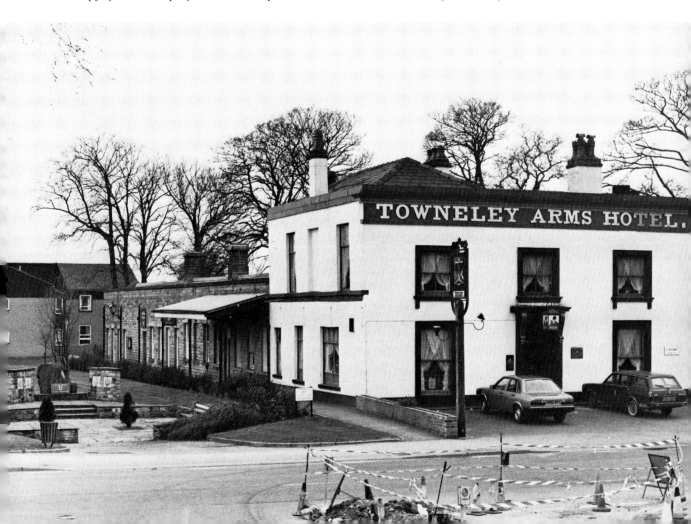

A view from the window of Chatburn on the Hellifield to Blackburn branch reveals a spick and span station with an open footbridge. The li closed to regular passenger services on 10 September 1962 but is still used for diversions and ramblers' trains. The station still exists. Photograph by M.A. Jose.

The Holcombe Brook branch had a chequered career, having been electrified on two differen systems and then returne steam working. In this photograph, taken during early BR days, the electri rails are still in position b the service is steam work by a L&Y 2-4-2 tank. T line closed to passengers 5 May 1952 having been de-electrified on 24 Marc 1951. Freight services la until 2 May 1960 when line was cut back to Tottington. Today, most the line is a footpath and Holcombe Brook station has been built over. Phot by C.H.A. Townley.

e Lancashire & Yorkshire Railway, along with the London & North Western, pioneered the use of railmotors referred to as "motor cars" in adshaw. The idea was to compete with tramway and motor bus services in suburban and rural areas, but the railmotors were not powerful ugh to take on extra coaches when the trains were crowded. Railmotors were displaced by conventional locomotives working "push & pull". 10609. seen here at Horwich on 25 July 1937, is awaiting scrapping, having been built in 1907. Photograph by N. Glover. The short rwich branch closed to passengers on 27 September 1965.

The famous Lancashire & Yorkshire Railway 2-4-2 tanks worked all over the system and featured on many branch line trains. Here a 2-4-2 belts uphill near Ilex Hall Carr on the now abandoned Bacup line. Photograph by C.H.A. Townley.

Middleton in LMS days, with class 4, 2-6-4T No 2282 and LMS maroon stock. Middleton closed to passengers on 7 September 1964 and freight on 11 October 1965. Middleton Junction has recently been renamed Middleton, the site at the original Middleton having now been built over and occupied by Crown Wallpapers who use it as their distribution depot.

Royton with an LMS class 4, 2-6-4 tank and a selection of pre-grouping stock. The leading vehicle looks as though it originated from the LNWR. The branch, which was only 1¼ miles in length, closed to all traffic on 18 April 1966. Photograph by C.H.A. Townley.

The Rochdale to Whitworth branch was traversed by an LCGB railtour on 19 February 1967, the locomotive being a Lancashire & Yorkshire Railway "pug" 0-4-0ST. The engine was built at Horwich in 1901 and has been preserved since 1965. The train did three trips up the Whitworth branch and the location is probably Wardleworth. The line closed completely on 21 August 1967.

LOCKWOOD TO MELTHAM
The Lockwood to Meltham branch of 3½ miles was opened for passengers on 5 July 1869. The branch had two intermediate stations at Netherton and Healey House but there was a third station at Woodfield, near the junction with the main line. Woodfield was opened in 1874 and was closed within a month — one of the shortest lived stations ever. The 1922 Bradshaw shows 10 trains per day on the branch with three extra on Saturdays and one extra on Tuesdays. Passenger services were withdrawn on 23 May 1949 and freight on 5 April 1965.

The present station buildings at Meltham are still in use as offices. Netherton station site is now a farmyard; Healey House station has been demolished and the site is a nature reserve owned by the local council.

BROCKHOLES TO HOLMFIRTH
This L&YR branch of 1¾ miles was opened on 1 July 1850, closed on 3 December 1865, and reopened on 11 March 1867. BR closed the branch on 2 November 1959 to passengers and 3 May 1965 to goods. There was one intermediate station at Thongs Bridge. The break in service from 1865 to 1867 was caused by the collapse of a viaduct at Mytholmbridge. Holmfirth station building is a superb stone Gothic structure converted into a private residence. Thongs Bridge station site has been filled in.

SHEPLEY TO CLAYTON WEST
Clayton West, last of the trio of Huddersfield–Penistone branches, was opened by the L&YR on 1 September 1879. There was one intermediate station at Skelmanthorpe and the line was 3½ miles long. The L&YR intended to extend the line to link up with the main line north of Barnsley, but with the opening of the Horbury Fork extension was not deemed necessary. Clayton West was an amazing survival into the present age and unlike Meltham and Holmfirth lasted well into BR days, even being dieselised in 1959. Passenger services were eventually withdrawn on 24 January 1983. By the spring of 1987 the track had been lifted back to the junction.

During the Beeching era of BR several attempts were made to close down the Clayton West branch but objections were always found as a suitable method of alternative transport was not forthcoming. The author purchased a Lancashire & Yorkshire Railway dog ticket at Clayton West in 1956 numbered 099; it may have been the last L&YR ticket to have survived into BR days.

DARTON TO SILKSTONE
The main line from Barnsley to Horbury was opened to goods on 15 January 1850 and the 1¾ mile branch to Silkstone was opened on the same day. The Silkstone (L&YR) branch was for minerals only and closed on 15 December 1937.

ROTHERHAM WESTGATE TO HOLMES JUNCTION
The short ¾-mile Rotherham Westgate branch closed to all traffic on 6 October 1952. This curious line came about as a result of being the first railway on the local scene, having opened on 1 November 1838. The Sheffield & Rotherham Railway, an isolated railway until joined to the North Midland in 1840, ran from Rotherham Westgate to Sheffield Wicker which was used for passengers until 1 February 1870. BR used Wicker Goods until 12 July 1965.

Photographs of Westgate are rare but the branch was visited by railtours on occasions. The site today is very difficult to find but has been occupied by the Rotherham postal sorting office. The passenger service over the nearby Chesterfield (Tapton Jcn) to Rotherham (Masborough) line, the original Stephenson route of the North Midland avoiding Sheffield, was withdrawn on 5 July 1954.

THE DEARNE VALLEY RAILWAY
HEMSWORTH (H&B) (BRIERLEY JCN) TO ROSSINGTON GN/GE (LOVERSALL CARR JCN)
The Dearne Valley Railway was financed by the colliery owners of Hickleton Main, Houghton Main and Carlton Main collieries and was opened in sections commencing with Brierley Jcn to Houghton on 19 March 1902. The final piece of the line was opened for coal traffic to Loversall Carr and Bessacarr Jcns on 17 May 1909. The railway was unusual in that it changed its allegiance, having been worked by the Hull & Barnsley from the outset but later entering into an agreement with the L&YR — changing sides from the East Coast Group to the West Coast Group. From 1923 the railway became part of the LMS instead of the LNER. There was a passenger service which was introduced by the L&YR on 3 June 1912, from Wakefield Kirkgate to Edlington Halt (Doncaster). The L&YR used their steam railmotor units and served track level halts. The units had fold-down steps for passengers, as on the GER and GWR. The L&YR steam railmotors gave way to LMS push and pull units and the final operation by BR ended on 10 September 1951. The service was worked by LMS Ivatt class 2, 2-6-2Ts at closure, and freight traffic was withdrawn on 11 July 1966 when BR put in a connection to the Midland main line at Houghton to serve the colliery at Grimethorpe.

RAILWAYS IN THE BARNSLEY AREA

The former passenger station at Barnsley Court House was closed to passengers on 19 April 1960 and trains diverted to the former Exchange station. The passenger service from Barnsley Court House to Cudworth (South Jcn) was withdrawn on 8 June 1958. Passenger services on the former main line from Normanton to Swinton ceased on 7 October 1968. Oaks Colliery to Monk Bretton and the Cudworth South curve closed to all traffic on 9 June 1958, the same day as the passenger service. The Rockingham Colliery branch closed on 22 July 1962, and Stairfoot Jcn to Cudworth South Jcn was closed to passengers on 7 September 1964.

ROYSTON TO DEWSBURY AND HUDDERSFIELD (NEWTOWN)

The Midland Railway proposed to extend to Huddersfield and put Bradford on a through route to Scotland via the Settle & Carlisle line. The Midland opened Royston Jcn to Thornhill on 1 July 1909. The two intermediate stations at Crigglestone and Middlestown never opened, the only local passenger service was provided by L&YR trains. The MR opened a 2½ mile branch to Dewsbury (Savile Town) to goods on 1 March 1906 but this line closed on 18 December 1950. The MR acquired running powers over the L&YR from Thornhill to Bradford and Leeds, the company having a scheme for a grandiose hotel and terminus at Huddersfield. The Huddersfield terminus never materialised, but the 4½-mile long Newtown Goods branch was built and used from 1 November 1910. The LMS opened a connection at Red Doles Jcn on 1 October 1923, thus shortening the former Midland line.

Mirfield Jcn to Red Doles closed on 12 August 1937 and Red Doles Jcn to Newtown on 5 August 1968. The Midland never got beyond Huddersfield. Royston Jcn to Thornhill closed to all traffic on 4 May 1968 having been used by summer Saturday trains after regular passenger workings ceased on 13 June 1960. Crigglestone viaduct of 21 arches still survives.

HUDDERSFIELD TO KIRKBURTON

The Kirkburton branch of 4¼ miles opened to passengers on 7 October 1867 and closed on 28 July 1930. The freight service lasted until 5 April 1965. There were intermediate stations at Deighton, Kirkheaton, and Fenay Bridge & Lepton. The LNWR introduced railmotors in 1916 which lasted until the passenger closure. The passenger service became a casualty of motor bus competition during the late 1920s. Little remains to be seen today of the line as all the stations have been demolished. Kirkburton station site has now been built upon. Deighton to Kirkburton Branch Jcn lasted until 12 December 1981 to serve the ICI works. Deighton is not to be confused with the modern halt of that name on the main line of Huddersfield.

BRADLEY WOOD JCN TO WYKE & NORWOOD GREEN (PICKLE BRIDGE BRANCH)

This 3¾ mile section of line with two stations at Brighouse Clifton Road and Bailiff Bridge closed to passengers on 14 September 1931 and freight on 4 August 1952. The passenger service ran from Bradford Exchange to Huddersfield. The viaduct at Wyke became unsafe and was a contributory factor to closure.

LOW MOOR TO MIRFIELD (L&YR SPEN VALLEY)

The main line from Manchester Oldham Road to Normanton was opened in 1840 via Mirfield as the Manchester & Leeds Railway, later to become part of the Lancashire & Yorkshire. The branch from Mirfield to Low Moor (7¾ miles) followed on 18 July 1848 and, after the costly construction of Bowling tunnel, access was gained to Bradford. The 2½ mile Heckmondwike to Thornhill section was opened to passengers on 1 June 1869 but closed to passengers on 1 January 1962. Low Moor to Mirfield closed to passengers on 14 June 1965, the section from Mirfield to Heckmondwike being to all traffic. Liversedge LNWR (Hargreaves) to Thornhill remains open for oil trains via a new LYR–LNWR spur installed in 1966 at Cleckheaton. The track from Cleckheaton on to Low Moor remains in place, is not used and has been singled. There is a plan for this latter section of line to be converted for tramway operation, but at present little progress has been made. The basic service during pre-LMS days was from Bradford to Dewsbury Market Place (the L&YR terminus).

The former Midland Railway ran a through service from Bradford to St Pancras via this route and Thornhill to Royston Jcn at one time. Low Moor to Cleckheaton ceased to be used by freight trains after 21 June 1971. The situation today is that Cleckheaton station has been demolished but a walk commences here and runs alongside the single unused track to Liversedge. The station buildings at Liversedge have been demolished but the goods shed survives.

At Heckmondwike the buildings have been demolished, but a large overgrown space awaits the developer near the station site. This is where planners hope a big shopping precinct and tram terminus will be constructed. At Ravensthorpe, the single track runs through to the junction with the main line; this station, or what remains of it, is not included in the tramway plans. West Yorkshire County Council hoped to take over the line at a cost of £3 million (1983 prices), electrify on the overhead system and run a tramway system with a service of preserved trams. The trams are stored and ready for use — only the finance and legalities are holding up this project. One of the objectors to the scheme was the nearby Keighley & Worth Valley Railway.

GREETLAND TO STAINLAND

This short L&YR branch of 1½ miles was opened for passengers on 1 January 1875 and closed to passengers on 23 September 1929. Goods traffic lasted until BR days and was withdrawn on 14 September 1959. The L&YR introduced a steam railmotor service on 1 March 1907 and opened a new halt at Rochdale Road just after the junction from the main line and between there and West Vale station. Tram competition and the growth of local bus services killed off passenger patronage in the 1920s and Stainland, like neighbouring Rishworth, suffered an early demise. The hilly nature of Stainland meant that much of the town was at a much higher altitude than the station, making for difficulty of access.

Stainland today is now occupied by a chemical factory, the trackbed being used by the factory's lorries. The line was built as a double track main line, as the intention of the L&YR was to extend to Littleborough to shorten the Calder Valley route.

BATLEY TO BIRSTAL (LNWR)

Birstal was served by a branch line from Batley and was opened on 30 September 1852, with one intermediate station at Carlinghow opened on 1 April 1872, the line being 2 miles long. Passenger services were withdrawn on 1 January 1917 as a war-time economy but freight lasted until 18 June 1962. The line was originally intended to go through to Bradford to compete with the nearby GNR and L&YR routes, but the GNR got there first via Upper Batley.

The line today has mostly disappeared and the terminus at Birstal has been built over. Part of the line is now a footpath between Wilton Park and Carlinghow. An overbridge exists in Wilton Park — probably the only engineering structure left to be seen today.

EARBY TO BARNOLDSDWICK (LANCASHIRE SINCE 1974)

This 1¾-mile long branch was a true branch line in that it served the local community and used nearly pensioned-off rolling stock and motive power, although the final steam services were worked by BR class 2, 2-6-2 tanks. The line was opened on 8 February 1871 as the Barnoldswick Railway, Lancashire & Yorkshire Railway locomotives gave way to BR standard tanks, the line closing as a steam-worked push and pull service on 27 September 1965. Goods traffic ceased on 1 August 1966, and the terminus at "Barney" — as it was known by the locals — is now the town car park. A quaint operation at the terminus was the Midland crossbar shunt signal which survived until BR days, and the run round of the train engine which involved the closure of the crossing to road traffic.

SOWERBY BRIDGE TO RISHWORTH

The 3¾ mile line from Sowerby Bridge to Rishworth opened to Ripponden on 5 August 1878, and Rishworth 1 March 1881 for passengers. The railway was part of the L&YR system until incorporated into the LNWR in 1922. The L&YR introduced a railmotor service in 1907 and opened an intermediate halt between Sowerby Bridge and Triangle (opened 1885) known as Watsons Crossing Halt. At Sowerby Bridge, the branch trains started from a platform well separated from the main station by the branch tunnel mouth. The railmotor service consisted of 18 trains per day at the Grouping but the service was withdrawn on 8 July 1929 — this dramatic decline being brought about by severe bus competition in the 1920s. The bus service to nearby Halifax served the villages door to door on the main road (A672), whilst the railway was situated on the other side of the river Ryburn and isolated. Freight services were withdrawn on 12 February 1953 from Rishworth, and back from Ripponden to Sowerby Bridge on 1 September 1958. The line was railtoured by an SLS/MLS special worked by an L&Y 2-4-2T prior to complete closure.

Today the trackbed is overgrown and Ripponden station site is now occupied by a housing estate.

RAWDON JUNCTION TO YEADON

This miniscule branch line of the former Midland Railway was just over one mile in length and never had a regular passenger service. Starting life as the Guisley, Yeadon & Rawdon Railway, the intention of the promoters was to construct a line to Headingley and provide an alternative route to Leeds. When the money ran out the Midland stepped in and opened it only as far as Yeadon on 1 June 1893. Rawdon Jcn commemorates the extension that never was. The line closed during wartime in 1944 but was not finally closed to all traffic until 10 August 1964. Yeadon did have occasional passenger trains, as seaside excursions were run to Morecambe and Blackpool during the summer.

Little remains to be seen today of this minor branch, and the Yeadon station site is now occupied by the local council as a depot.

KEIGHLEY TO OXENHOPE (K&WVR)

The Keighley & Worth Valley Railway opened on 15 April 1867 as an independent railway but was taken over by the Midland at a later date. The branch was 4¾ miles long and included stations at Ingrow, Damens, Oakworth, Haworth and Oxenhope. Passenger services by BR were withdrawn on 1 January 1962 and freight on 18 June 1962. The line, having been closed under

BR, was typical of many minor branch lines to be eliminated during the sixties — but the K&WVR proved to be different. The railway was relatively short to operate, passed through pleasant scenery and had a good tourist potential at Haworth with the Brontë parsonage. In addition to the tourist potential, the railway was situated near a large centre of population, i.e. the West Riding, from where day trippers could visit in large numbers.

On 1 March 1962 the Keighley & Worth Valley Railway Preservation Society was formed at a meeting, and professional railwaymen, local businessmen and enthusiasts were recruited. The K&WVRPS was not the first standard gauge line to be preserved, but was one of the earliest. As a result of being an "early preserved railway", the K&WVR took some time to reopen, the BR solicitor claiming that it was the first time that BR had sold a line back to private ownership. The contract for purchase by the Keighley & Worth Valley Light Railway Company was signed on 6 April 1967. The railway was reopened to the public on 29 June 1968, six years after closure, such are the technicalities and legal obstacles that railway preservationists have to endure.

Since reopening, the railway has gone from strength to strength, many historic locomotives and rolling stock have been purchased and an intensive service run in the summer months. Of interest is the station at Ingrow with the buildings transferred, brick by brick (or stone by stone), from Foulridge and the tiny station at Damens — reputed to be the smallest on the former Midland system. At Oakworth the station has been restored to Midland colours with chocolate and cream paintwork and red doors. At Haworth and Oxenhope the buildings are restored to London Midland Region red and cream colours. The railway has featured in many films, TV ads and plays, the most famous being "The Railway Children" — mainly based at Oakworth and Mytholmes tunnel. The railway today is one of the most successful of Britain's operating private railways.

SKIPTON TO COLNE
The line was opened by the Leeds & Bradford Extension Railway on 2 October 1848 and was the first railway to Colne, later being leased to the Midland and becoming part of that company's system. Colne became a "frontier town" between the Midland and Lancashire & Yorkshire, although the L&Y had running powers to Skipton and worked the passenger service. The passenger and freight services were withdrawn on 2 February 1970 between Skipton and Colne. Of the intermediate stations, Elslack was closed on 3 March 1952 and Foulridge on 5 January 1959. Of the stations today, Elslack (in LMS colours) is used for storing tractors, Thornton-in-Craven has been demolished, Earby is occupied by a warehouse and Foulridge has been taken apart bit by bit to be reassembled at Ingrow on the Worth Valley line. A footpath is being laid out along the trackbed from Colne to Earby, a distance of 6½ miles. Colne remains as a branch terminus with a service to Blackburn and Preston.

THE YORKSHIRE DALES RAILWAY
The Yorkshire Dales Railway Museum Trust at Embsay station had a dogged start, as the preservationists wanted to take over the Grassington branch but were thwarted because the quarry at Rylstone (Swinden) did not close. The stone trains from Swinden Quarry still operate via Skipton and BR track. The Yorkshire Dales opened to the public on 19 May 1979. The objective for the YDR is now Bolton Abbey, but there are problems including an overbridge which BR still owns, and land which has been sold off near Bolton Abbey.

The Yorkshire Dales Railway has a comprehensive collection of locomotives and rolling stock. There is also much pre-grouping equipment and one of the most well-stocked railway bookshops anywhere. The bookshop is an "Aladdin's Cave" of obscure railway titles, and the YDR claim to have every railway book that is in print in Britain in stock. The railway operates at weekends during the summer months, from Easter until late September. There are also special weekend firework displays near November 5th, and of course Santa trains during December weekends. There is an impressive selection of locomotives, totalling 22 in all — mostly steam — and all industrial, according to the 1983 stock book. The railway manages to exude a spirit of notable enthusiasm and sociability.

SHIPLEY TO ILKLEY (O&I)
Ilkley, of Otley and Ilkley Joint fame, is still open to passengers, being a terminal station with a frequent service of trains from Leeds and Bradford. The town was served by the Midland from Leeds via Apperley Jcn, and the North Eastern via Otley, and opened on 1 August 1865. The section from Otley via Burley in Wharfedale to Ilkley was jointly owned between the Midland and North Eastern railways. The line was known as the Otley & Ilkley Joint Railway, being served by the Midland from Bradford, Shipley and Leeds direct from 4 December 1876.

SKIPTON TO GRASSINGTON & THRESHFIELD
The Grassington branch from Skipton via Embsay Junction was opened as the Yorkshire Dales Railway in 1902 but was worked by the Midland from the start of operations. The YDR was planned to extend to Darlington but the finance was not forthcoming. The 10¾ miles from Skipton to Grassington passed through rural countryside, there being only one intermediate station at Rylstone, 3¼ miles from Grassington. The Midland passenger service of 1922 consisted of seven trains per day each

way. The LMS withdrew this service on 22 September 1930 but Sunday excursions ran well into BR days. BR withdrew freight from Grassington on 11 August 1969, but the line is still open to Swinden Tilcon quarry, near Rylstone. Grassington station has been built upon, the housing estate being known as "Piece Fields".

SKIPTON TO ILKLEY

The Midland branch from Skipton to Ilkley was opened to the public on 1 October 1888, the Midland station at Ilkley being alongside the terminal (O&I) station. The Otley & Ilkley Joint station at Ilkley, which is still in use, was one of the last gas-lit stations on BR. The line passed through the Yorkshire Dales and was popular with excursionists, Bolton Abbey being a well-known tourist attraction. The line was often patronised by royalty, who visited Bolton Hall. The line was dieselised during the 1960s, using multiple unit trains from Bradford Forster Square. During the final days of steam working there was a good variety of locomotive types to be found working the line, as there were through freight trains from the North Eastern Region. Passenger services were withdrawn on 22 March 1965 and freight on 5 July 1965. The track has been lifted but part of the line is now being reopened by the Yorkshire Dales Railway who operate from Embsay and hope to extend to Bolton Abbey — a rather decrepit wooden building in faded North Eastern Region colours.

CLAPHAM TO LOW GILL

This railway could have been part of the main line system of Britain, had events turned out differently. The line was built between the two great railway systems, the Midland and the LNWR. The Midland was determined to expand northwards into Scotland and the LNWR was equally determined to prevent Midland expansion. The railway started out in life as the "little" North Western Railway and was opened from Clapham to Ingleton on 30 July 1849. The Ingleton branch was closed on 1 June 1850 with the opening of the through route from Skipton to Lancaster. One presumes that the "little" North Western Railway did not have enough motive power or rolling stock to run both lines! The Clapham to Ingleton section reopened to passengers on 1 October 1861.

Ingleton to Low Gill was constructed by the LNWR and opened for passengers on 16 September 1861, the LNWR having its own station at Ingleton on the other side of Ingleton viaduct from the Midland's station. The Midland acquired the "little" North Western but the two rival companies ignored one another, hence two stations at Ingleton. Passenger trains did not connect and passengers making through journeys had to walk between the two stations. The situation was only relieved in 1917 when the LNWR station, known as Ingleton (Thornton) was closed. When the LMS was formed in 1923, the line came under one owner and proved to be a useful route for diverted West Coast main line trains. The route was used for engineers' works diversions for passenger or freight well into BR days.

The passenger service was withdrawn on 1 February 1954, and freight on 19 June 1966. Diversions ran until 26 July 1966, the line being used for many Sundays when the West Coast main line was blocked for engineering works. The railway ran through a scenic part of the country and can easily be traced today. The viaducts at Ingleton and Low Gill can still be seen. The demise of this line has probably saved the nearby Settle & Carlisle route from extinction.

GARSDALE TO HAWES

The Midland had a short branch from Garsdale on the Settle & Carlisle line to Hawes where the line joined up with the Wensleydale branch of the North Eastern. The line was opened on 1 October 1878 and closed to all traffic by BR on 16 March 1959. The railway was six miles in length and at closure only had one train per day. Much of the course of the line is still visible from the main road. Garsdale was well known for the stockaded locomotive turntable made out of old sleepers. Garsdale to Appersett viaduct, a distance of 5 miles, is to be converted into a footpath. Hawes station and goods shed survive, tastefully restored and used as a local tourist information office.

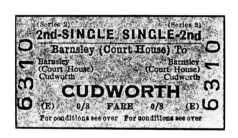

Hawes was an outpost of the Midland and the North Eastern Railways. Some Midland characteristics survive in this 1959 photograph, such as the fence, the seat, and the oil lamp hut near the bridge. The lamps on the platform are North Eastern. The station was jointly owned and the 6 mile branch to Garsdale closed to all traffic on 16 March 1959. Most of the route is to be converted into a foot and cycle path.

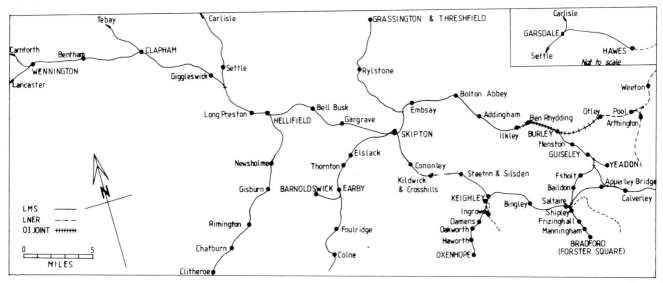

Scenes on the Yorkshire Dales Railway, with Bolton Abbey station on 22 August 1965, hopefully the ultimate goal of the preserved YDR. The scene below shows the present scene at Embsay with 0-6-0ST No 7 in steam. Embsay station also has a well stocked bookshop.

Rotherham Westgate passenger station was owned by the Midland Railway, being the successors to the Sheffield & Rotherham Railway which was the first railway to arrive on the scene in 1838. The North Midland to Masborough did not arrive in Rotherham until 1840, hence the two terminals. Rotherham Westgate closed to passenger and freight traffic on 6 October 1952. The locomotive is a Johnson 0-4-4T dating from the 1880s.

Grassington, with 4F No 44220 pushing back the empty stock of an excursion from Colne in 1961. The line closed to regular passenger traffic on 22 September 1930, but Sunday ramblers excursions ran for many years afterwards. The Grassington to Rylstone section did not close until 11 August 1969. Most of the line is still in use to Rylstone from Skipton.

The rise and fall of a Pennine branch line — Clayton West in 1965 with a through train to Huddersfield in the upper picture contrasts with today's dereliction seen in the lower.

The impressive gothic architecture at Holmfirth still survives as the station buildings are now a house, although the railway closed to all traffic on 3 May 1965. Upper photo by C.H.A. Townley, lower by Lens of Sutton.

The battered remains of the station nameboard Ripponden & Barkisland rest on the platform whilst the SLS/MLS railtour makes a brief pause on its way to Rishworth with the last train in February 1953. Passenger services were withdrawn as early as 8 July 1929 and freight on 12 February 1953. A housing estate occupies the site. Photograph by C.H.A. Townley.

Stainland, with the SLS/MLS railtour in February 1953 shows a L&YR 2-4-2T running round the train. Stainland closed to passengers on 23 September 1929 and freight on 14 September 1959. The site is now a private road used by lorries. Photograph by C.H.A. Townley.

Barnoldswick (upper picture) on a miserable wet September day with standard tank No 84015 about to depart on the last train to Earby. The station is now part of the town car park, photographed by Hugh Ballantyne on 25 September 1965. In the lower picture can be seen train on the Dearne Valley line on 23 April 1949 at Grimethorpe. The L&YR railmotor had vacuum operated fold down steps and L&Y 2-4-2 tank No 10647. Note the low platform and LMS livery of the L&Y saloon. Photograph by C.H.A. Townley.

THE CROMFORD & HIGH PEAK RAILWAY

The Cromford & High Peak Railway which ran from High Peak Jcn on the Midland main line, between Ambergate and Matlock, to Ladmanlow and Whaley Bridge was unique. The railway was opened throughout in 1831 and was laid out by Josiah Jessop, the canal engineer. The line was built from Cromford Wharf, where a connection was made with the Cromford Canal, to Whaley Bridge on the Peak Forest Canal — a distance of 33 miles. The Peak Forest Canal connection from Shallcross, near Whaley Bridge, to Ladmanlow closed to all traffic in 1892. Ladmanlow to the private sidings at Harpurhill closed to all traffic on 2 August 1954. The principal traffic conveyed on the line was limestone from the various quarries along the route which was noted for its steep inclines and tortuous curves. The system of steep inclines with winding houses worked by stationary engines and continuous chains was used instead of lock flights which would normally be in use on a canal. The route was originally conceived as a canal but The Railway Age came into being during planning. One incline with 60 yards at 1 in 14, Hopton, was worked by locomotives until closure in 1967 and was the steepest adhesion worked incline in Britain. The railway was horse worked on the level stretches until 1840, although horses were still at work on the Whaley Bridge to Shallcross section until 1952. Two parts of the railway incredibly survived until 1 May 1967 under BR ownership. There was a passenger service until 1877 and during the final years special railtours were organised by railway clubs, utilising open wagons for passengers. The passenger service, which ceased in 1877, only consisted of one train per day and was terminated after a runaway on one of the inclines.

There is still plenty to see today as the line has been turned into a footpath known as the "High Peak Trail". The distance is 17½ miles and the footpath, which caters for cyclists, walkers and equestrians, is maintained by Derbyshire County Council. Of the sights to see today are the engine shed and workshops at High Peak Junction near Cromford Wharf, Sheep Pasture engine house, Middleton Top engine, Hopton incline, and the site of Longcliffe station including the goods shed. At Middleton Top, cycles can be hired from the Derbyshire County Council's Visitor Centre. Motive power on the route has been just as fascinating as the railway itself, starting off with old LNWR types. The last Webb 2-4-0T No 58092 was in use on the line and the LMS introduced North London Railway 0-6-0 tanks which were themselves replaced by BR with ex LNER J94 "Austerity" tanks. LMS 0-4-0 saddletanks in the 47000 series were also used until ousted by diesels in August 1966. One North London tank survives (LNWR No 2650) which can still be seen at work today on the Bluebell Railway in Sussex — the engine dates from 1887.

ASHBOURNE TO BUXTON

The Ashbourne–Buxton line was an LNWR branch opened on 4 August 1899 from Ashbourne to Parsley Hay. It then used the rebuilt Cromford & High Peak line into Buxton's LNWR terminal, next door, and identical with that of the Midland. The LNWR provided a basic all-stations service between Buxton and Ashbourne and also, until 1916, a through service to Euston via the North Stafford Railway. The passenger service was withdrawn on 1 November 1954 from Buxton to Ashbourne but the section from Buxton to Hindlow is still used for stone from the quarries. Hindlow to Hartington closed to all traffic on 2 October 1967, with Hartington to Ashbourne closing completely on 7 October 1963.

The Ladmanlow branch of Cromford & High Peak fame closed completely on 2 August 1954.

The line, having been closed 20 years and the track lifted, is now walkable from Ashbourne to Dowlow along the "Tissington Trail", which joins the "High Peak Trail" at Parsley Hay. The "High Peak Trail" is to be extended over the Ladmanlow branch and onto Whaley Bridge from Harpur Hill — a distance of 9½ miles. Derbyshire County Council also have cycle hire centres at Ashbourne, Parsley Hay, and Middleton Top. Hire of a cycle presently costs £3.20 per day and is the best way to see the closed branches. There are one or two relics to be seen such as gradient posts and the odd milepost, while the signalbox at Hartington has been well restored.

DUFFIELD TO WIRKSWORTH

The Midland Railway ran an 8½ mile long branch from Duffield to Wirksworth, with through trains to Derby. Opened on 1 October 1867, the line had three intermediate stations and is still available to take trains, the passenger service having been withdrawn on 1 January 1949. The Wirksworth branch had a healthy freight business until recently with stone trains to Barham and seasonal sugar beet to Kings Lynn. The stations still survive and have been converted into private houses. Idridgehay has a solar-powered ungated automatic level crossing — quite an unusual feature on a British line. A development in recent years has been the reintroduction of the passenger service on Spring Bank Holidays for the Wirksworth Well Dressing Festival. The line may not last for much longer as the existing traffic is seasonal, and may be withdrawn. The Well Dressing specials ran on 23/25 May 1987.

RIPLEY TO DERBY AND LANGLEY MILL & EASTWOOD

The Midland opened Ripley to Butterley (now on the preserved line) and Ripley to Heanor on 2 June 1890. The line was extended on to the main Erewash Valley line at Heanor Jcn on 10 October 1895. As far as is known, there was no passenger service from Heanor to the junction, the passenger service being worked from Butterley to a separate branch platform at Langley

Mill & Eastwood (now Langley Mill). The present Langley Mill station is of course new, opened as recently as 12 May 1986, the old station having closed on 2 January 1967. There was no connection between the Langley Mill branch platform and the present main line. The service from Butterley to Langley Mill was withdrawn on 4 May 1926, the section from Heanor to Butterley being to all traffic. Ripley continued to be served by direct trains from Derby. As far as can be ascertained, the Langley Mill to Heanor spur closed completely, to the passenger service in 1926. The Heanor Jcn to Heanor goods section closed to all traffic on 1 September 1951. Heanor to Ripley was used for wagon storage for a year or so after closure, until 1928. Butterley to Ripley closed to all traffic from 25 November 1929 and track began to be removed in 1938.

Ripley was first served by a direct branch from Little Eaton Jcn opened on 1 September 1856. The line was built on the course of the plateway known as the Little Eaton Gangway (from the Derby Canal). The passenger service from Ripley to Derby was withdrawn on 1 June 1930, but freight continued from Ripley to Marehay Crossing until 1 April 1963 and from there to Denby North until 29 July 1968. Denby southwards to Little Eaton Jcn is still used for coal trains. Ripley station today has been obliterated by in-filling, although the road bridge over the former station is still in situ and a footpath exists through the station site.

AMBERGATE TO PYE BRIDGE

The 6½ mile Ambergate to Pye Bridge line passed through Butterley, today's headquarters of the Midland Railway Centre. Passenger services commenced on 1 May 1875 and continued until 16 June 1947. The line had opened to freight on 1 February 1875, there being several colliery lines in the area including the privately owned Butterley Company system. Freight traffic ceased on 23 December 1968.

Since closure, work has proceeded on a preservation scheme on the Codnor Park to Swanwick Sidings and Hammersmith section of the line. Much rolling stock has been gathered of Midland and LMS origin and regular trains are run on summer weekends. The Midland Railway Trust, originating from 1969, was assisted by the County Council. In 1979 Derbyshire County Council purchased the line from Butterley (Hammersmith, at the end of the reservoir) to Pye Bridge.

Since then, a large shed has been erected to house museum exhibits at Swanwick Jcn. The station building from Whitwell has been re-erected to form Butterley station and many artefacts of the Midland Railway have been collected. A grant from the English Tourist Board for construction of the museum was forthcoming and a Light Railway order was granted on 27 July 1981, the official opening date being 22 August 1981.

Prize exhibits on the line are the Kirtley 2-4-0 No 158A of 1866, Johnson single No 673 of 1897, and LMS 4F No 4027 of 1924, on loan from the National Collection. There is also at present the Somerset & Dorset 2-8-0 No 13809, some 1F and 3F 0-6-0Ts and a "Peak" class diesel-electric No D4. Codnor Park to Ironville Loop is still in situ for transfer of locos and rolling stock, as well as occasional through excursion passenger trains.

ILKESTON TOWN BRANCH

The short ¾ mile Ilkeston line opened on 6 September 1847 to passengers, the same day as the Midland main line through the Erewash Valley. The line was not very well patronised and was closed in 1870, but re-opened on 1 July 1879 to compete with the newly opened GNR Nottingham to Derby line. The passenger service lasted until 16 June 1947 when withdrawn by the LMS. Freight lasted under BR until 22 August 1964 and the station site has now been built upon.

KIMBERLEY (BENNERLEY JCN) TO BASFORD JCN

The Midland Railway opened the Kimberley branch in stages from 1877 to 1882, the last section to Bennerley Jcn on 13 October 1879 for goods and 1 September 1882 for passengers. The line duplicated the newly opened GNR Nottingham to Derby line and passenger services were withdrawn on 1 January 1917. The section from Kimberley to Digby Branch Jcn closed to all traffic on 1 January 1917, goods lasting until 1 February 1954 on the Kimberley to Basford Jcn section.

ELMTON & CRESSWELL TO STAVELEY TOWN

This part of the former Midland Railway's network in the North Derbyshire coalfield still flourishes with trains serving the numerous collieries in the area and Seymour Junction marshalling yard. Passenger services on this section were withdrawn on 5 July 1954, the service being from Mansfield to Chesterfield. Summer Saturday trains ran under BR until 18 August 1962.

MANSFIELD TO STAVELEY TOWN VIA BOLSOVER

The passenger service from Mansfield to Chesterfield via Bolsover and Staveley ceased on 28 July 1930, and it is likely that freight ceased between Glapwell and Pleasley on the same day. Bolsover Colliery Miners Welfare Institute have in recent years organised annual excursions to Cleethorpes in the summer. Glapwell Colliery closed in 1977, the official BR closure date for the section Bolsover to Glapwell to all traffic being 31 October 1978. Glapwell station to the colliery closed to freight in April 1959.

The tranquil scene at High Peak Junction Workshops where the Cromford & High Peak Railway met the Cromford Canal. The original workshops of the C&HPR are open to the public as a museum run by Derbyshire County Council. There is an exhibition of the railway which was built by a canal engineer in 1831 and lasted under BR ownership until 1967. The railway was noted for its very steep inclines which were cable worked. The Hopton incline was as steep as 1 in 14 but was worked by locomotives. This was the steepest worked locomotive used incline in Britain.

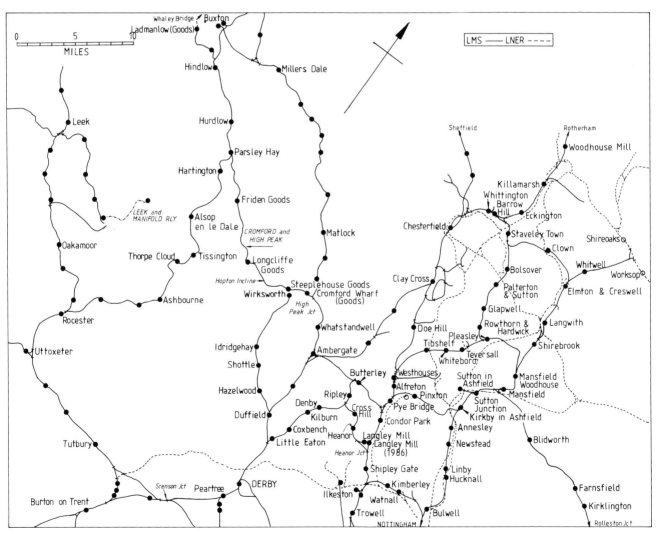

Ambergate, in the upper picture, was unusual in that it was one of Britain's few triangular stations. Middleton Top in the lower picture shows two North London Railway tanks on a special on 21st May 1955. Photo by H. Ballantyne, and M.A. Jose (upper).

Wirksworth in Midland days with private owner wagons and heavy mineral traffic in the sidings. The stone from the nearby quarry was conveyed until recently by BR. The limestone was used in sugar beet factories. Photograph by Lens of Sutton (upper). In the centre picture, Wirksworth station today — a scene greatly changed from Midland days. The future of the line may now be in doubt. The Well Dressing specials were the last passenger trains.

Idridgehay station on the now closed Wirksworth branch is unique. The station still exists although the regular passenger service was withdrawn on 16 June 1947 just before nationalisation. The station at Idridgehay is now a private house with the ungated crossing being protected by colour light signalling operated by solar panels. The system is in use in continental Europe but only used here in Britain as an experiment. As freight trains no longer run to Wirksworth, the future of the signalling scheme is very much in doubt.

MANSFIELD TO ALFRETON VIA TEVERSALL

The thrice daily passenger service over this section in Midland days was from Mansfield to Pye Bridge and was withdrawn by the LMS on 28 July 1930, the same day as on the Pleasley–Staveley line. Freight traffic still runs to Silverhill and Sutton collieries, the section from Pleasley to Teversall having closed to all traffic from 18 July 1981. Mansfield Woodhouse (Pleasley Jcn) to Hollins Siding closed to all traffic on 3 March 1964, and Hollins Siding to Pleasley Colliery on 4 January 1965.

PYE BRIDGE TO MANSFIELD AND WORKSOP

The present freight-only line from Pye Bridge to Shirebrook and on to Worksop on the main Sheffield to Lincolnshire line serves as an outlet for 16 collieries. The former LDEC and GCR lines have been connected at Shirebrook Jcn to this former Midland route. The coal traffic flows northwards to Tinsley or southwards to Toton. Passenger services were withdrawn over the Pye Bridge to Kirkby-in-Ashfield section on 10 September 1951, although a workmen's service continued until 6 September 1965. Kirkby-in-Ashfield to Worksop passenger services ceased on 12 October 1964, thus depriving Mansfield, once a centre for numerous passenger services, of all passenger trains. Mansfield, with a population of 53,000, is now one of the largest towns in Britain without a rail passenger service. The nearest station is 8 miles away at Alfreton & Mansfield Parkway. This station was reopened by BR on 7 May 1973 and at first provided Mansfield with a fast inter-city service to London or Sheffield. Patronage did not come up to expectations, partly due to the slow bus link with Mansfield; and Mansfield now has a fast bus service to Newark on the East Coast Main Line. The present service consists of one up and one down HST, the rest being sprinters.

NOTTINGHAM (RADFORD JCN) TO KIRKBY-IN-ASHFIELD (LEEN VALLEY)

The Leen Valley was remarkable in that no less than three railways, the Midland, Great Northern, and Great Central, all had their own lines along the valley. All were built to tap the lucrative coal traffic. Today, only one line, from Radford Jcn to Hucknall, with a modern spur to Calverton colliery, serves the area, BR having sensibly rationalised the duplication in the area. The Midland was the first line to Mansfield, opened to Kirkby-in-Ashfield on 2 October 1848 and on to Mansfield on 9 October 1849. The Midland bought out the Mansfield and Pinxton railway and opened as a tramroad in 1819. The passenger service from Nottingham to Mansfield via the Leen Valley ceased to run on 12 October 1964. The track of the former Midland line is now lifted south of Kirkby-in-Ashfield, having ceased to be used to Annesley Colliery Jcn on 12 October 1970. Linby Colliery is served by the line southwards to Radford Jcn. The Newstead Colliery to Linby section closed from 8 August 1983 to all traffic, following Newstead Colliery to Annesley Colliery on 25 February 1980. Linby Colliery closed on 19 March 1988.

SUTTON-IN-ASHFIELD TO SUTTON JCN

This short ¾ mile branch was opened on 1 May 1893 and closed to passengers in 1917, reopening in 1923 and closing again on 26 September 1949. A workmen's service was run until 10 October 1951 when the line closed to all traffic. The stub end of the line was used for wagon storage until 1971. The building at Sutton-in-Ashfield is still in use as a bus garage, and at the Sutton Jcn end of the line a Midland Railway signalbox survives. The former Midland route south of Sutton Jcn was diverted in 1972 onto the course of the old GNR line for about one mile to avoid level crossings, new connections being put in by BR at each end of the GNR section.

ROLLESTON JCN TO SOUTHWELL AND MANSFIELD

Mansfield to Southwell opened on 3 April 1871 providing an eastern outlet from the Nottinghamshire coalfield. Passenger services were few, the 1922 Bradshaw showing only two trains per day with an extra train on Saturdays. The Southwell to Rolleston section had 20 trains per day. Passenger services over the Mansfield Town to Southwell section were withdrawn on 12 August 1929, the Southwell to Rolleston section lasting until 15 June 1959 for passengers. Freight ceased to run from Blidworth Jcn to Southwell on 1 March 1965 and Southwell to Rolleston Jcn on 2 May 1966. Today, Southwell's fine "Midland Railway neo-Gothic" building survives as a private house, surrounded by modern development. A recent development is the "Southwell Trail" from Farnsfield to Southwell, a 4½ mile footpath along the railway trackbed, on which Kirklington and Farnsfield stations are now private houses. Southwell station in its heyday and right up to the mid-fifties was the epitome of the Midland country branch line, with Midland, signals, motive power and architecture. The Rolleston Jcn–Southwell "push & pull" train was the last service worked regularly by a Midland Railway class IP 0-4-4T.

LEICESTER TO BURTON (INCLUDING THE LEICESTER & SWANNINGTON RAILWAY)

The present Leicester to Burton line, which closed to passengers on 7 September 1964, continues to thrive on coal traffic from the Leicestershire coalfield, though colliery production in the area is expected to cease by 1990. The railway runs partly over the original course of the Leicester & Swannington Railway of 1832. The colliery owners of West Leicestershire were looking for an outlet for their coal, the Charnwood Forest Canal reservoir having burst its banks, and having been generally an unsatisfactory route, using tramroads part-way.

The success of railways for coal hauling in the north led to the coal owners seeking advice from George & Robert Stephenson in 1828. The result was the opening of the first section from Leicester West Bridge to Bagworth on 17 July 1832. This was one of the earliest steam-hauled railways and as a result had a few peculiarities not associated with latter-day railways. The Midland Railway acquired the line in 1846 and modernised it, building a new line from Leicester to Desford, thus creating the West Bridge branch, and building a deviation around the 1 in 29 Bagworth incline. The Midland also extended the line to Burton from Coalville on 1 August 1849.

The Leicester & Swannington had a passenger service from the day of opening and being a pioneer railway did not use platforms, passengers having to join the train from ground level. Tickets were also issued at public houses, the railway reserving accommodation for this practice in the inns where passengers would wait. The concept of the railway station as we know it had not yet arrived here. The railway had two steep cable worked inclines at Bagworth and Swannington while the nearly 1 mile long Glenfield tunnel had no manhole recesses. The tunnel was provided with gates at each end to keep the unwary public out. A few of these relics can be seen today, including the tunnel entrance at Glenfield and the inclines at Bagworth and Swannington. The stationary winding engine at Swannington, dating from 1833, was removed to York Railway Museum in 1952. Passenger services over the West Bridge line were withdrawn by the LMS on 24 September 1928 and freight by BR on 2 May 1966.

The Leicester & Swannington is also where the steam engine whistle is reputed to have been invented in 1833 (locomotives prior to that date carried bells, a practice perpetuated in the Americas).

THE LEICESTER & SWANNINGTON LINE TODAY

Leicester West Bridge station site is now a public park and nature trail. The Local Authority have built a miniature station on the site of the 1893 Midland station and even a station nameboard. A plaque reminds visitors that the station was in use until 1966. The work was completed in 1986 by the Manpower Services Commission. At Glenfield there is a modern housing estate entitled "Stephenson Court", and tucked away at the back of this estate is the entrance to Glenfield tunnel. Ratby station has been demolished, as also has Kirby Muxloe, but Desford station buildings still stand. At Bagworth the incline can be seen, and at Bardon Hill there is a fine old Midland signal box but no station. Coalville and Swannington stations are now demolished but the pub "The Station" commemorates the building. Ashby station is now used as offices and is well preserved, being in the "Grecian style" — the Burton & Ashby Light Railway 3'6" gauge track can still be seen in the forecourt. Moira Station buildings still exist but are in a bad state of repair, being painted in faded BR (LMR) red and cream colours. Moira West Jcn has a superb Midland Railway signalbox. The line was singled from Moira West Jcn to Mantle Lane from 14 December 1986, reflecting the run-down of coal traffic on this section. The Swannington incline was last used on 14 November 1947 but is now reported as proposed for conversion to a footpath.

SWADLINCOTE LOOP LINE

Following the completion of the Leicester to Burton line in 1849, a branch line to Swadlincote was constructed in 1864 to serve the collieries and potteries. The Swadlincote branch was extended to a terminus at Woodville in 1883 and connected back to the main line in 1884, thus creating the complete loop. Passenger services were withdrawn on 6 October 1947, but excursion traffic and summer Saturday trains continued until 8 September 1962. The loop line closed in stages, from Cadley Hill Colliery being still open to Swadlincote Jcn. Cadley Hill to Swadlincote closed to all traffic from 2 March 1964. This section of line was used to store wagons until 26 August 1968. Swadlincote to Woodville Goods was closed to all traffic from 2 March 1964. The station at Swadlincote has been demolished but the platform edges can still be seen in a new housing development.

ASHBY & NUNEATON JOINT RAILWAY

The sections of line Moira to Nuneaton, and Coalville (Hugglescote) to Shackestone, were jointly owned by the Midland and LNWR and opened on 1 September 1873. The passenger train service became Ashby to Nuneaton for Midland trains and Loughborough to Nuneaton for LNWR trains. The LMS withdrew the passenger service on both lines on 13 April 1931, but excursions did run to Skegness until 1961. An excursion poster is on display in the Shackestone Museum. Freight traffic ceased from Shackestone to Hugglescote on 6 April 1964, the section from Measham to Market Bosworth being closed to all traffic on 12 November 1971, and Market Bosworth to Nuneaton on 19 July 1971. A short section at Hugglescote reopened about 1976 as part of the new rail link to Coalfield Farm open cast site loading point. This also included: (a) LNWR spur from the Leicester–Burton line; (b) new spur into Coalfields Farm, a British Coal conveyor belt on 3 miles of track bed from Coalfields Farm to Ibstock. All of this is currently in use. Measham & Donisthorpe Colliery to Overseal (the top end of the joint line) closed to all traffic on 20 June 1981.

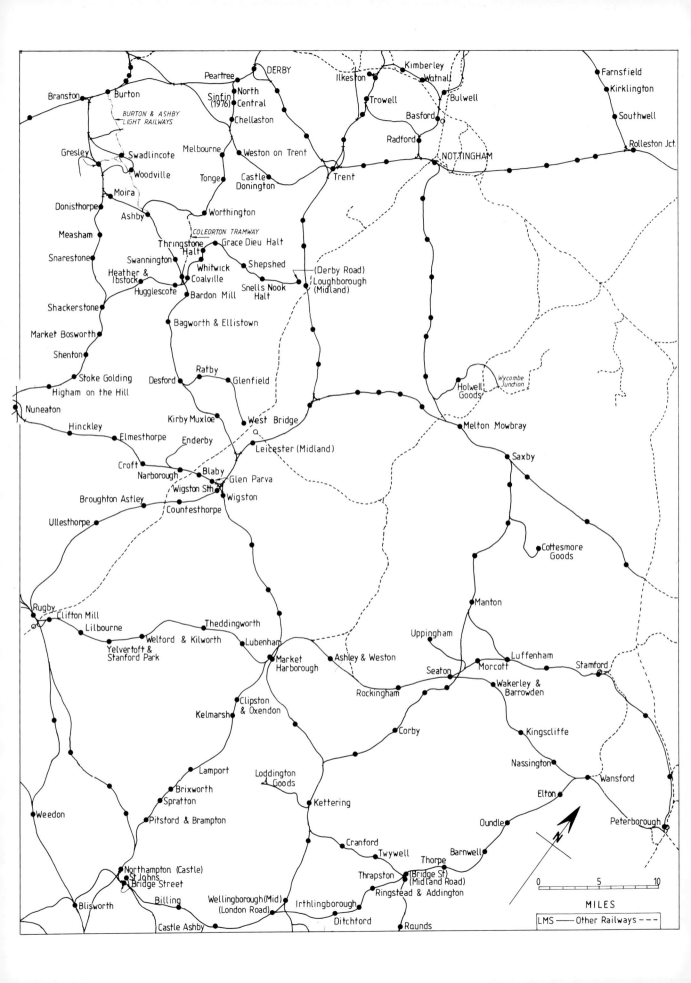

NARBOROUGH TO ENDERBY

The LNWR main line to Nuneaton from Leicester had a branch from Narborough to Enderby built to serve the granite quarries and opened in 1890. The line was jointly owned between the LNWR and Midland companies. Traffic ceased by 1976 but official closure date was 30 April 1980. The line was 2½ miles long.

SHACKERSTONE RAILWAY SOCIETY (MARKET BOSWORTH LIGHT RAILWAY)

Following the cessation of freight traffic on the Ashby and Nuneaton Joint Railway from 1971, a railway society was formed to reopen the stretch from Shackerstone to Market Bosworth. An accumulation of locomotives, rolling stock, and signalling relics meant that services could recommence on 26 March 1978 between Shackerstone and Market Bosworth. The railway society hopes to extend the regular service to Shenton where a restored railway station awaits them. Shenton station is at the Bosworth battlefield site and is an ideal destination for travellers from Shackerstone. The railway has a collection of 0-4-0 and 0-6-0 industrial tanks, a few ex-industrial diesels and some secondhand BR coaches to work the service. The service runs from Easter until the end of September, on Sundays and Bank Holidays.

Shackerstone station is situated in a rural area and approached along a gravel roadway lined with trees and running parallel to the Ashby Canal. The trees are reputed to have been planted at the request of Earl Howe of Gopsall Hall. The station was used by King Edward VII in 1906, who was unable to get out of the Royal Train at the appointed spot because the platform had been raised. Today, Shackerstone station is being restored to BR red and cream colours; there is a refreshment room, shop and museum. The museum is an Aladdin's Cave for railway enthusiasts and is crammed full of many historic relics. The collection of railwayana has been accumulated by J. Jacques who started work at the station at the age of 14. Mr Jacques is still employed by BR as a signalman. The railway museum is looked after by John Blake, a retired miner, who studiously lights the oil lamps and stokes a coal fire, giving the station a touch of authenticity. Stoke Golding station is now a private house, and Higham-on-the-Hill is demolished, although the station master's house still exists. Snarestone station is now in use for boarding dogs, Measham station is used by a car repairer and Donisthorpe is demolished.

LOUGHBOROUGH DERBY ROAD TO SHACKERSTONE

The London & North Western Railway built a branch to Loughborough from the Ashby & Nuneaton joint line at Hugglescote which was opened in 1883. The service operated by the LNWR was from Loughborough to Shackerstone where connection was made with Midland trains from Moira. Connection was also made with the MR Burton to Leicester line at Coalville — the LNWR did have its own station at Coalville (East) and operated a rail motor on the Loughborough branch. There were intermediate halts at Thringstone, Grace Dieu and Snell's Nook. The LNWR were pioneers in opening unstaffed halts on branch lines. Loughborough (Derby Road) to Shackerstone closed to passengers on 13 April 1931, freight being withdrawn from Loughborough to Shepshed on 30 November 1955, although wagons were stored on the line for some years after closure. Coalville East to Shepshed closed completely on 11 December 1963. The section of line from Coalville to Hugglescote closed to all traffic on 17 August 1964.

The line today has a few relics to show but the station at Hugglescote has been demolished and the goods yard built upon. Heather & Ibstock is also demolished but the station house survives — "Station Terrace" commemorates the railway. At Coalville East, the LNWR station's site has been built upon and is now an industrial estate — the name "Old Station Close" commemorates the LNWR's existence. At Whitwick the station buildings have been tastefully restored by an MSC grant and are painted in LMS/LMR maroon and cream, and the trackbed is a footpath to Coalville. At Shepshed, another "Old Station Close" appears where the railway once ran on Shepshed industrial estate. The LNWR terminus at Loughborough Derby Road has disappeared but there is the "Station Hotel", "Station Street", and even "Station Avenue". A Jet petrol station dominates the site and the goods shed is now a motor coach depot.

THE BURTON & ASHBY LIGHT RAILWAYS

The Midland empire stretched to distant parts of Britain and included canals, shipping, docks and hotels, but the most unusual part of this vast undertaking was the Burton & Ashby Light Railways. The Burton & Ashby Light was in fact an inter-urban tramway of a type popular in North America and similar to today's Manx Electric Railway. The light railway was owned by the Midland and operated as a subsidiary company, a major railway company operating electric trams being an unusual arrangement. The Midland could see the danger of Burton Corporation extending the town's tramway system towards Swadlincote and Ashby, thus threatening revenue from the Midland's own existing stations on the Burton to Leicester line and the Swadlincote loop.

The trams started running from Ashby-de-la-Zouch to Burton-on-Trent on 2 July 1906. The distance was 10 miles and the journey took 1 hour 20 minutes. The gauge was 3′6″ and 20 open top cars were provided for the line. A branch to Gresley was opened on 24 September 1906. The cars were finished in Midland livery of crimson lake and off-white with the Midland Railway coat of arms on the lower deck side panels. The tramway was operated on a 550 volt DC overhead system and ran on its own right of way through the country areas. A connecting line from Woodville to Gresley operated until November 1912. As usual with pre-war light railways and branch lines, motor buses took the traffic and the Burton & Ashby closed down to all traffic on 19 February 1927. What a wonderful tourist attraction the Burton & Ashby would have made today, had it survived.

A few relics can be seen today, some surviving pole bases and inspection hatches can be discerned along the course of the line, but the best in situ relic is the original track in the station approach at Ashby-de-la-Zouch. The workshops at Swadlincote are currently in use by British Coal. As recently as 1980, one of the tram cars (No 14) was renovated and sent to the United States where, on the Detroit Citizen's Railway, the car runs (adapted to metre gauge) for tourists and rail fans. The most eminent rider on No 14 having been no lesser person than Ronald Reagan who in 1980 rode the car during the Republican Congress. The restoration of car No 14 is a story in itself. The body was found in a field at Church Gresley, little more than a rotting hulk when found, the car took many years to restore. A fitting testimony to the tenacity, patience and willingness of the restorers.

DERBY TO ASHBY VIA CHELLASTON AND MELBOURNE
This route has had a chequered history which at the current time of writing has yet to be completed. Formerly a Midland through route to the coalfields of South Derbyshire, the line Peartree to Chellaston Jcn only had one intermediate station known to the Midland as Chellaston & Swarkstone. The Midland had services from Derby to Ashby and also from Trent via Chellaston to Derby. The growth of local motorbus services in the 1920s and 1930s killed off local rail passenger traffic in the Derby area and services were withdrawn on 22 September 1930. Chellaston closed to goods traffic on 13 June 1966 and Peartree (Melbourne Jcn) to Chellaston Jcn to all traffic on 30 December 1973, the track south of Sinfin being lifted in 1974.

On the section from Chellaston Jcn (renamed by BR to Worthington Jcn) to Ashby passenger services ceased to function from 22 September 1930. The army took over the line during World War II when it was known as the Melbourne Military Railway. BR closed the section from New Lount to Ashby from 9 May 1955. Coal ceased to be conveyed from New Lount from 27 November 1968 and finally stone trains ceased to run from Worthington from 21 May 1980. The track to Worthington is still in place at the time of writing. The closure of the Worthington to Worthington Jcn section terminated the long history of rail transport from the limestone quarries in the area, going back to the days of the Ticknall Tramway and the Coleorton Railway. The Midland Railway acquired and built over part of the Ticknall Tramway from Worthington to Ashby-de-la-Zouch in 1874.

On 1 October 1976, the first train ran from Derby to Sinfin Central, a new station, marking the partial reopening of the line, with a new intermediate station at Sinfin North and a reopened Peartree. The line was reopened with a fairly heavy subsidy from Derbyshire County Council with the intention of taking commuter traffic off the roads. The scheme has not proved to be successful, and is now reduced to a service of three trains per day. Although the service is worked economically by using multiple unit diesel sets to fill in, with their crews, on the Matlock service, patronage is negligible. Sinfin North has no public access and Sinfin Central has an overgrown and lengthy footpath from the main road. The scheme has been criticised as only half implemented — had the line been reopened in full through to Chellaston and beyond, a through service would have attracted more custom. Today, Chellaston station buildings have been demolished but the station house survives. Melbourne has been demolished, Tonge & Breedon is a dog training centre, and Worthington is a private house, tastefully restored.

TRENT TO STENSON JCN
This line is still used as a freight and diversionary route for trains avoiding Derby, the passenger service to the two intermediate stations having been withdrawn on 22 September 1930. Castle Donington and Weston-on-Trent stations have been demolished but the station house survives at Weston.

RUGBY TO LEICESTER
This was one of the early trunk routes of the country, having opened as part of the Midland Counties Railway in 1840 being an extension from the London & Birmingham's main line at Rugby. This was the principal route to the North East prior to the construction of the East Coast Main Line. After the Midland had extended southwards from Leicester, this line became a secondary cross-country route. BR closed the line for passengers and freight on 1 January 1962. Of the stations on the line, Ullesthorpe is the most interesting as it is still complete and has been lovingly restored by its owners, Mr & Mrs Taylor, to LMS maroon and white colours. The old station is discreetly hidden in the middle of a modern housing estate. The other stations on the branch are demolished or built over. The pub at Countesthorpe, "The Railway", is worth a visit to see railway relics in all bars. Leire Halt was not one of the original stations but was constructed in 1925, the villagers having subscribed a sum of money to the LMS for its construction. A footpath, the "Jubilee Way", runs from the site of Leire Halt to Ullesthorpe.

BLISWORTH TO NORTHAMPTON (BRIDGE STREET)
The London & Birmingham Railway was opened throughout on 17 September 1838, passengers for Northampton having to change at Blisworth for a 4½ mile road journey to Northampton — Blisworth to Northampton (Bridge Street) not being connected for rail traffic until 13 May 1845. Northampton has been often called the town that missed the railway, as opposition from landowners was so strong to the building of the London & Birmingham line when proposed in 1830 that the town was

avoided, being served by a branch from Blisworth until the more direct line was constructed in 1882. The passenger service from Blisworth to Northampton Castle ceased on 4 January 1960 although the line was used until 3 January 1966 for diversions during electrification. Freight traffic lasted until 6 January 1969. Northampton (Bridge Street) to Briar Hill is still used for Tamping machine training.

NORTHAMPTON TO PETERBOROUGH

This cross-country line was opened as a branch of the London & Birmingham on 2 June 1845, being 43½ miles long and the first railway in the area, having been built well before the Midland main line or the Great Northern. After the construction of these two main lines the route became of secondary importance and closed to passengers on 4 May 1964. Freight trains were withdrawn from Northampton to Wellingborough on 1 August 1966. The sections of line Wellingborough to Irthingborough closed to freight on 6 June 1966; Irthingborough to Thrapston on 7 June 1965; Thrapston Bridge to Oundle on 4 May 1964; and Oundle to Peterborough on 6 November 1972. The latter part from Yarwell Junction to Peterborough has been retained for the Nene Valley Railway.

The present course of the line still has a few interesting relics, as most of the stations still survive in various guises. At Northampton Bridge Street the station has been demolished but the LNWR signal box still survives to serve the nearby engineers' depot. Of interest at this location is the LNWR goods warehouse, still in LMS colours of brown and black. This is probably the best surviving example of an LMS secondary building painting scheme that can be seen today and will be of interest to modellers. The first station along the branch is at Billing. The station buildings are occupied and known as "Billing Station House". Further along the closed line at the former Castle Ashby & Earls Barton, the traveller is confronted with Dunkleys Licensed Restaurant — Richard Dunkley was a local building contractor who built the Northampton to Market Harborough branch. The restaurant is in the former goods shed with two LMS coaches as an annexe, and the station house is a private residence. Wellingborough (LNW), Ditchford and Irthlingborough are demolished or obliterated, whilst Ringstead & Addington site is now occupied by a conveyor belt. Thrapston Bridge Street is a timber yard and Thorpe is now a nicely restored private residence with the platforms still in situ. Barnwell station is now inhabited by a former railway employee, but some of the platform buildings have been moved to the Nene Valley at Wansford. Barnwell has a verandah that used to house the LNWR frame. Oundle station is a superb stone gothic building awaiting restoration, and Elton has been demolished.

THE NENE VALLEY RAILWAY

The section of line from Wansford (Yarwell Jcn) to Peterborough has now been taken over by the Nene Valley Railway. The NVR run to their own terminus at Peterborough, opened to passengers by HRH Prince Edward on 30 June 1986. Peterborough NVR station is on the approximate site of the original L&BR station. The passenger service is from Wansford to Peterborough (NVR), some trains running via Yarwell Jcn, and operates from Easter until late September at weekends (daily from June to the end of August). In addition to the Nene Valley service, connecting trains operated from BR Peterborough (North) to Orton Mere on Saturdays during the summer. These trains were operated by BR until 28 June 1986.

The Nene Valley Railway is approximately 7 miles long, houses a unique collection of locomotives and rolling stock from 9 countries and specialises in running continental trains. The inaugural NVR train ran on 9 April 1974, the passenger service through to Orton Mere from Wansford commencing with a special on 1 June 1977. The present terminus at Peterborough is a bleak affair, 15 minutes walk and within sight of the BR station and the town centre. It is situated near the BR line from Peterborough to March, just before it passes under the GNR main line. There is no physical connection at that point with the BR tracks and the terminus can be seen from the main line when arriving from the south at Peterborough.

Locomotives on the railway include a Swedish 2-6-2T, 2-6-4T and 4-6-0, a French 4-6-0, a Danish 2-6-4T and 0-6-0T, a German 64 class 2-6-2T, and 80 class 0-6-0T, a 2-8-0 and a selection of continental coaches including Wagonlits. The railway also possesses some notable British locomotives and second hand coaches from BR (MK 1). BR locomotives include class 5MT 4-6-0 No 73050, 7MT 4-6-2 No 70000, and Bulleid 4-6-2 No 34081, an un-rebuilt version rescued from Barry scrapyard in 1975. The freight rolling stock is of interest and includes some items dating before the 1923 grouping. The railway features frequently in films and TV.

NORTHAMPTON TO MARKET HARBOROUGH

This line was opened on 16 February 1859 by the LNWR from Northampton Bridge Street to Market Harborough where connection was made with the LNWR Rugby to Seaton line. The line was built to keep the Midland from encroaching southwards from Market Harborough and ran through unspoilt rural countryside. The stations were not situated near any of the villages en route and passenger traffic was light. The line was useful as a through and diversionary route for both passengers and freight and although the regular passenger service was withdrawn on 4 January 1960, BR ran a through overnight train from 1969 until 1973. Freight ceased to run on 17 August 1981, although the overnight passenger train which BR introduced on 6 January 1969 lasted until 26 August 1973.

The track was lifted by the Spring of 1986 and very little remains to be seen of the stations today. Northampton County Council has bought the trackbed of the entire line from Pitsford northwards, and the line is at present being converted into a footpath and nature trail. At Market Harborough, the Up platform edge of the former LNWR station survives, and at Lamport the signalbox and station buildings survive in faded LMS green and cream, but the rest of the stations have been demolished.

At Pitsford the headquarters of the Northampton Steam Railway have been established. The Railway have purchased track and will relay ¾ mile of line and operate steam trains at weekends. An 0-6-0ST "Colwyn" ex-North Norfolk Railway, Kitson of 1933, an SR double-deck coach, a "Pullman", two diesel shunters, an LNWR signalbox and a lot of hope are the current assets. No doubt, with time the collection will grow.

RUGBY TO PETERBOROUGH AND STAMFORD

The LNWR opened Rugby to Luffenham on 2 June 1851, the line having been planned originally as a branch from the London & Birmingham main line. The section of line from Seaton, to join the existing Northampton to Peterborough branch of the former London & Birmingham, was opened by the LNWR on 1 November 1879. The line passed through thinly populated countryside and with the completion of the Midland main line to St Pancras and the East Coast main line through Peterborough, became a secondary cross-country route. The distance from Rugby to Peterborough was 50¾ miles. The BR timetable for 1965 shows 5 trains per day each way, one being through from Rugby to March, one being a Birmingham to Ely, and one running Birmingham to Lowestoft. Not all of these trains stopped at the intermediate stations, and Lilbourne, 3½ miles from Rugby, only had two trains per day with an additional train on Saturdays.

Passenger services were withdrawn from Rugby to Peterborough via Wansford, and Seaton to Luffenham on 6 June 1966. The Seaton to Luffenham line was worked by push and pull trains, the service being Seaton to Stamford Town, worked by an Ivatt class 2, 2-6-2T at closure. Between Seaton and Wansford and Seaton to Kingscliffe the sections were closed to all traffic on 6 June 1966, Kingscliffe to Nassington on 3 June 1968, and Nassington to Wansford (Yarwell Jcn) on 4 January 1971. Following closure of the Nassington Iron Stone Quarries, the last iron-stone line worked by steam traction, on 31 December 1970. The section from Yarwell Jcn to Peterborough is now operated by the Nene Valley Railway.

The Seaton to Luffenham line closed to all traffic on 6 June 1966, along with the section on to Market Harborough and Clifton Mill (Rugby). The only station on the Luffenham to Seaton section was at Morcott, which is now a timber yard. On the Wansford to Seaton section, Nassington and Kingscliffe stations have been demolished but the station houses are still lived in. Wakerley & Barrowden station still survives and is unusual in construction. The station buildings, with booking hall, are at ground level in brick, whilst the entrance to the platforms, at a higher level, is in LNWR timber. The station house is still in use and the whole building is in a reasonable state of preservation.

Seaton station buildings still survive and are used for a scrap motor business. The proprietor is renovating the building and repainting the timberwork in LMR red and cream. Seventeen layers of paint have been scraped off, going down to LNWR cream on oak originating from when the station was built — probably dating from 1879.

The next station along the line towards Market Harborough at Rockingham is also of interest as it still stands, having been converted into a dog breeding establishment. The name "Rockingham" painted in black letters across the actual building and probably dating from opening in 1851 is an extremely rare survival of the once-common early British practice of painting the name across the station buildings. The practice is common on US railroads and in New Zealand, but long defunct in Britain. Another rarity is at the former Ashley & Weston station which is now a branch of the Midland Bank.

On the Market Harborough to Rugby section, Lubenham has been demolished, Theddingworth is now a private house with the signalbox converted to a garage, and Welford & Kilworth has been flattened. Yelvertoft & Stamford Park is now the "Willows Country Club", a resort for anglers — the building having been well restored and extended. Lilbourne station buildings have been demolished but the platforms still exist and the crossing keeper's cottage is still lived in. Clifton Mill has been demolished.

SEATON TO UPPINGHAM

The Uppingham branch of the former London & North Western Railway, of 3¾ miles in length, was one of the best examples of the traditional English branch line. The line was opened on 1 October 1894 mainly to rival the nearby Midland main line station at Manton for Uppingham, but was not used by many people. The passenger service was withdrawn on 13 June 1960 and was worked by Ivatt 2-6-2Ts with a push and pull unit.

The line was well known for its use of Fowler 0-4-4Ts and the ex LTSR 4-4-2T No 41975 in the 1950s. Freight traffic was withdrawn on 1 June 1964.

The line was unusual in that to get to Uppingham the train had to cross the rival Midland main line twice to climb out of the Welland Valley. Uppingham station site is now an industrial estate.

THE RUTLAND RAILWAY MUSEUM (COTTESMORE BRANCH)

This BR mineral line closed on 2 December 1973, since when the upper end of the line has been operated as the Rutland Railway Museum. The Museum opens every weekend, has steam days on Bank Holiday weekends and possesses a large number of steam and diesel locomotives of industrial origin. There are also several goods and passenger vehicles of interest to the visitor. The Museum is organised using a mixture of volunteers, MSC grants, and county grants. The location near Rutland Water and the A1 is ideal for visitors and day trippers.

The rolling stock includes Wisbech & Upwell coaches, pre-grouping vehicles, and the star attraction, an 0-4-0ST named "Singapore" built by Hawthorns in 1936. This locomotive was at Chatham Dockyard until recently and came from Singapore where it spent the war years — the locomotive still has the bullet holes in the boiler casing as a relic from that time. Another feature of the Rutland Railway Museum is the Nature Trail which shows examples of wild flowers usually to be found by the trackside on railways, open or closed.

HOLWELL JCN TO WYCOMBE JCN (THE HOLWELL BRANCH)

This line was opened by the Midland Railway in 1876 (Ashfordby Jcn—Holwell) and extended to Wycombe Jcn in 1887 to convey iron ore from Waltham-on-the-Wold. The line was closed to freight trains from 27 July 1963.

WELLINGBOROUGH TO HIGHAM FERRERS

This line was opened to freight traffic on 1 September 1893 and passengers on 1 May 1894 by the Midland Railway, following local pressure from the growing towns of Rushden and Higham Ferrers. Local industry was expanding and the Midland provided double track earthworks and intended to extend the line from Higham Ferrers to Raunds to join up with the Kettering—Huntingdon branch. This line was not built, so the branch terminated short at Higham and was single track throughout. Passenger services were withdrawn on 15 June 1959 and freight lasted until 3 November 1969. The line was traversed by a railtour on 18 May 1968, which is believed to have been the last passenger train and was organised by the Railway Correspondence & Travel Society. In its heyday the passenger service was worked by Midland 0-4-4 tanks, later displaced by BR class 2, 2-6-2s in the 84000 series. Not much can be seen at Higham Ferrers today as the station and goods shed have been demolished, but when the visitor gets to Rushden he is in for a very big surprise! Rushden station, which was closed in 1959, is complete and in use. The station has been restored to LMS/LMR livery which is red and cream, the platform nameboards, seats, and advertisements have been replaced and the refreshment room reopened as a restaurant. The whole operation has been carried out by the Rushden Historical Transport Society who occupy the building on a three year lease. They have purchased a Midland Railway signalbox for £350 and the station bar even has draught beer pumps — anything seems possible nowadays!

KETTERING TO LODDINGTON

This was a Midland mineral line from Kettering and was eventually disused by 22 June 1970. The Midland Railway opened the line in 1891 to convey iron ore. Loddington had a metre gauge industrial system which connected with the standard gauge MR branch. Loddington Quarries closed on 6 July 1963.

KETTERING TO CORBY

Not really a branch line, this, as the line is on the route of the former Midland main line from Nottingham to Kettering via Oakham. Part is still used for diversions when the main line via Market Harborough is blocked. The former main line between Edwalton and Melton Mowbray is used by BR as a test track. The section from Melton Jcn to Manton Jcn is still used by Leicester to Peterborough trains and Corby to Glendon South Jcn was reopened to passengers on 13 April 1987. Corby to Kettering was originally closed by BR to passengers on 1 May 1967. After 20 years without passenger trains, Corby, one of the largest rail-less towns in the country, is now back on the BR map!

KETTERING TO HUNTINGDON

The Midland Railway ran a service from Kettering to Cambridge via the Great Eastern through Huntingdon East and St Ives. The MR owned the first 27½ miles to Huntingdon and the line opened on 27 February 1866 to goods and 1 March 1866 to passengers. The line was single throughout and included sidings to quarries to tap the ironstone traffic between Kettering and Thrapston. The passenger service was sparse, being 4 through trains in Midland days and 3 under BR until closure, which took place on 15 June 1959. The freight service was withdrawn from Huntingdon to Kimbolton on 15 June 1959, from Kimbolton to Twywell on 28 October 1963 and Twywell to Kettering on 20 March 1978. The line ran through unspoilt agricultural country and possessed some picturesque stations.

From Huntingdon to Kettering there are some interesting relics still to be seen today. At Buckden the station still exists as a complete entity, having been bought and lived in by a local enthusiast, Mr S. J. Smith. The station is complete with Midland signalbox, weighbridge hut, and even the firebucket rack, and the buildings are still in their green and cream colours. At Grafham the former station is now the Post Office, and at Kimbolton the station has recently been restored by a local builder who has made an excellent job of turning the former station into a private house. The builder is not however a railway engineer, as he would not have put the lamp-posts so near to the platform edge. Raunds station is now a private house and Thrapston (Midland Road) is now Thrapston Agricultural Services Ltd. Thrapston station buildings, goods shed, and even the Midland signalbox are still extant. Twywell and Cranford stations are now private houses.

Southwell station buildings survive but have now been converted into a private house, squeezed into a modern housing development. The Midland Railway fence and crossing gatepost survive in this modern scene.

Wigston South on 12 August 1961 with the 5.40 pm Leicester (London Rd) to Rugby Midland behind 2-6-4T No 42062 (upper picture). A fine Midland Railway signalbox and gaslamps complete the vintage scene. Photograph by Hugh Ballantyne.

Leire Halt on the Leicester to Rugby line was not one of the original stations on the line as it was opened on 4 April 1925 after pressure from the villagers upon the LMS to provide a station. Leire Halt was partly built at the expense of the local community. The line was opened as the Midland Counties main line in 1840. In the top picture class 4, 2-6-4 T arrives to collect passengers whilst in the lower a youthful Mike Jose awaits salvation. The line closed to all traffic on 1 January 1962. Photographs by M.A. Jose.

The changing scene at Ullesthorpe, showing the station which had staggered platform in 1960 (above) and 26 years later in 1986. Not much has changed except that the track has gone and the building has now been converted to a private house in LMS colours!

Heyday of the Leicester West Bridge branch seen in Midland days in the upper picture with 0-6-0 and six-wheelers. In the picture below, a facsimile station has been reconstructed near the site of the Midland station. The reconstruction was carried out by the local authority under a Manpower Services scheme. Upper photo by Lens of Sutton.

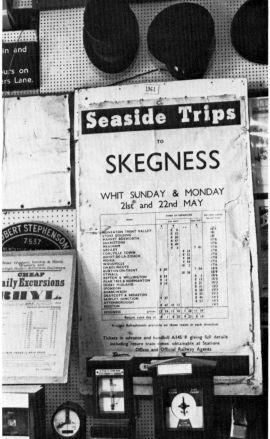

Market Bosworth station as seen today with the multiple unit in the platform (upper) and a view of an excursion poster to Skegness inside the museum. The poster is surrounded by old signalling equipment and stationmasters' top hats. In the lower picture the staff is being exchanged at Woodville on the Swadlincote Loop. Photograph by J.R. Langford.

Shepshed, on the Loughborough Derby Rd branch with a railtour in 1957 organised by the REC. The Midland 3F 0-6-0 is working tender first in the upper picture and the locals have turned out to see a passenger train on the line that closed to passengers on 13 April 1931. Note the LNWR lamp. In the lower photograph taken in 1951, the passenger station is in good condition even after 20 years of closure. Freight trains ceased to run on 11 December 1963. The site is now occupied by an industrial estate. Photo by Real Photographs.

Buckden in 1987 looking very much like Buckden in 1959 (seen below) — some things never change! The present building is complete with signal box and outhouses. The Midland Railway fence remains in situ, even the television aerial is still unaltered. The line was closed completely on 15 June 1959.

Buckden in 1959 — nearly 30 years separate the photographs but there has not been much change! The oil lamps have gone, along with the Midland seat, but the signal box of Midland origin survives. The single track branch of the former Midland Railway was a through route from Kettering to Cambridge. Photograph taken on 26 March 1959.

Raunds, as viewed by a passenger from the 11.20 am Cambridge to Kettering on 11 April 1959. The rolling stock is in the BR standard post 1948 red & cream colours discontinued after 1956. Children play on the platform as no passengers come for the train. Passenger services on the Cambridge to Kettering line ceased from 15 June 1959. Raunds still exists as a private house. Photograph by J.R. Langford.

A classic branch line scene at Olney (above) on the Northampton to Bedford branch of the former Midland Railway with engine & brake departing: note the turntable behind the fence. The line closed to passenger traffic on 5 March 1962 and freight on 6 January 1964. Photograph by M. Jose. Below, a Midland signalbox still survives at Thrapston.

Uppingham, in the long scorching hot summer of 1959 with an LMS push and pull unit and Fowler 0-4-4T in the upper photograph. In the lower photograph, class 2 2-6-2 No 41212 pauses at Ketton & Collyweston with the Seaton to Stamford push & pull. Photograph by M. Wilkins.

BR standard class 5 4-6-0 No 73050 "City of Peterborough" steams into Ferry Meadows on the Nene Valley Railway, a stretch of railway which once formed the London & Birmingham Railway's through route from London to Peterborough. Ferry Meadows was opened in 1978 by the Nene Valley Railway and was used in a James Bond film, but the site was once occupied by Overton, opened in 1845.

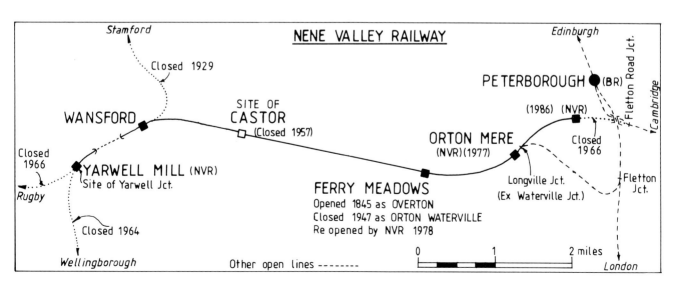

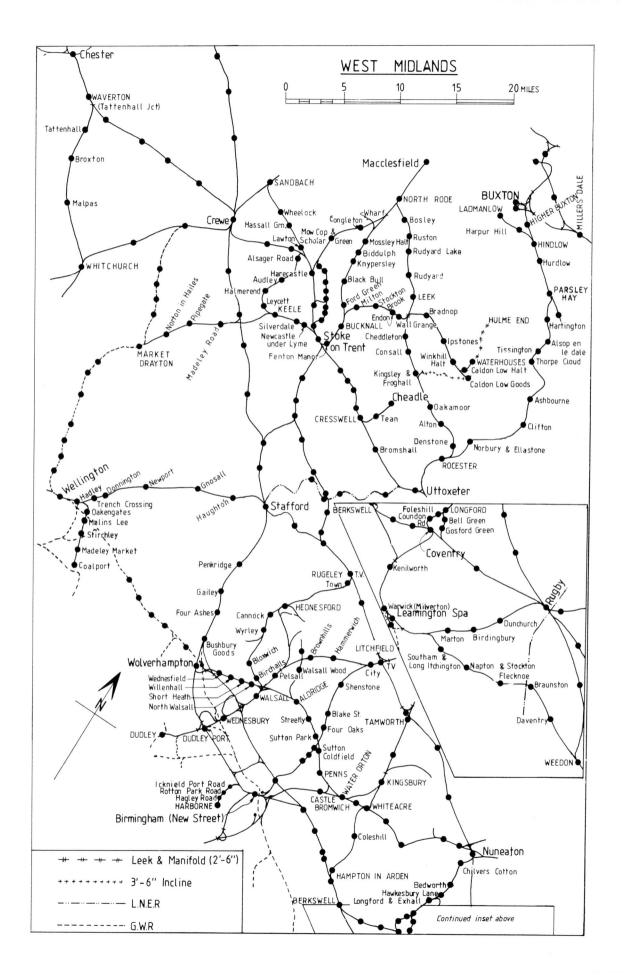

WEST MIDLANDS

0 5 10 15 20 MILES

Chester
WAVERTON
(Tattenhall Jct)
Tattenhall
Broxton
Malpas
Crewe
WHITCHURCH
Norton in Hales
Pipegate
MARKET
DRAYTON
Madeley Road
Wellington
Hadley
Donnington
Newport
Gnosall
Trench Crossing
Oakengates
Malins Lee
Stirchley
Madeley Market
Coalport
Haughton

SANDBACH
Wheelock
Hassall Grn
Lawton
Mow Cop &
Scholar Green
Alsager Road
Audley
Harecastle
Halmerend
Leycett
KEELE
Silverdale
Newcastle
under Lyme
Fenton Manor
Macclesfield
NORTH RODE
Congleton
Wharf
Bosley
Mossley Halt
Biddulph
Knypersley
Black Bull
Ford Green
Milton
Stockton
Brook
BUCKNALL
Stoke
on Trent
Cheddleton
Consall
Ruston
Rudyard Lake
Rudyard
LEEK
Bradnop
Wall Grange
Ipstones
Winkhill
Halt
Kingsley &
Froghall
Caldon Low Halt
Caldon Low Goods

BUXTON
LADMANLOW
HIGHER BUXTON
MILLERS DALE
Harpur Hill
HINDLOW
Hurdlow
PARSLEY
HAY
Hartington
HULME END
Alsop en
le dale
Tissington
Thorpe Cloud
WATERHOUSES
Ashbourne
Clifton
Norbury & Ellastone
ROCESTER
Uttoxeter
Cheadle
Oakamoor
Tean
Alton
Denstone
CRESSWELL
Bromshall

Stafford
BERKSWELL
Foleshill
Coundon
Rd
LONGFORD
Bell Green
Gosford Green
Coventry
Kenilworth
Rugby
Penkridge
RUGELEY
Town
T.V.
Dunchurch
Gailey
Four Ashes
Cannock
Wyrley
HEDNESFORD
Bushbury
Goods
Bloxwich
Birchalls
Pelsal
Walsall Wood
City
Brownhills
Hammerwich
LITCHFIELD
TV
Warwick (Milverton)
Leamington Spa
Marton
Birdingbury
Southam &
Long Itchington
Napton & Stockton
Flecknoe
Braunston
Daventry
WEEDON
Wolverhampton
Wednesfield
Willenhall
Short Heath
North Walsall
WALSALL
ALDRIDGE
Shenstone
Streetly
Blake St.
Four Oaks
TAMWORTH
WEDNESBURY
DUDLEY
DUDLEY PORT
Sutton Park
Sutton
Coldfield
PENNS
WATER ORTON
KINGSBURY
Icknield Port Road
Rotton Park Road
Hagley Road
HARBORNE
Birmingham (New Street)
CASTLE
BROMWICH
WHITEACRE
Coleshill
Nuneaton
Chilvers Cotton
HAMPTON IN ARDEN
Bedworth
Hawkesbury Lane
BERKSWELL
Longford & Exhall
Continued inset above

N

Leek & Manifold (2'-6")
3'-6" Incline
L.N.E.R
G.W.R

66

WEEDON TO LEAMINGTON

The first section of the line from Weedon to Daventry, a distance of 3¾ miles, was opened on 1 March 1888. The line was completed on to Marton Jcn where it joined up with the Rugby line on 1 August 1895. The single line was worked by LNWR engines and the Webb 2-4-2 tanks were replaced eventually by Ivatt class 2, 2-6-2s working on push and pull units. Steam working lasted until closure to passengers on 15 September 1958.

Freight services ceased from Weedon to Napton on 2 December 1963, and Napton to Southam on 5 November 1962. Southam & Long Itchington was used from then on by cement trains to Rugby which ran to Marton Jcn and reversed to travel to Rugby via Dunchurch; this arrangement was in force until March 1985. The line was specifically kept open for the cement traffic but BR failed to negotiate a new contract for it. The last known train was an inspection train on 17 July 1985 — BR officially closed the line from 1 August 1985 and lifted it in 1987.

The station buildings at Southam have been demolished, as also have Napton & Stockton, Flecknoe and Braunston, but Braunston railway houses remain near the site. Daventry has been obliterated by a road scheme, but a footpath exists along the trackbed to Braunston.

LEAMINGTON TO RUGBY

The line from Leamington to Rugby was opened by the LNWR on 1 March 1851; the LNWR were anxious over intrusion into their territory by the GWR who had their main line running through Leamington Spa from 1852. The LNWR had a separate station alongside the GWR, called Leamington Spa (Avenue), which has since been demolished. The passenger service from Leamington Spa to Rugby was withdrawn on 15 June 1959. The Leamington to Marton Jcn section was closed to freight on 4 April 1966. Trains have not run from Southam since March 1985 and the track was lifted in 1987. The line was worked by LMS 2-6-2Ts until closure to passengers in 1959.

Of the stations on the line, Dunchurch, Birdingbury and Marton all still exist. Dunchurch and Birdingbury have been converted into private houses, while Marton is in use by a plant and equipment firm.

LEAMINGTON SPA TO COVENTRY AND BERKSWELL

The first railway to Leamington was opened by the London & Birmingham Railway on 9 December 1844 to Leamington Spa Milverton; there was only one intermediate station at Kenilworth. The short cut off route from Kenilworth Jcn to Berkswell opened to all traffic on 2 June 1884. Under the Beeching regime the passenger service from Leamington to Coventry and Berkswell was withdrawn on 18 January 1965. In May 1966, BR improved the connection at Leamington Spa North to accommodate increased freight which had been diverted off of the former Great Central line. With the opening of Birmingham International in January 1976, Inter City trains were diverted via Kenilworth and Coventry from 2 May 1977, thus reintroducing a passenger service.

The line is now part of a main line Inter City route and has been promoted from branch line status. Kenilworth Jcn to Berkswell closed to freight on 17 January 1969 and is to be turned into a footpath, the track having been lifted. There are one or two fine London & Birmingham bridges to be seen on the line although Kenilworth station has been demolished recently.

COVENTRY TO NUNEATON

Coventry to Nuneaton opened on 12 September 1850, the London & Birmingham having opened through Coventry on 9 April 1838. The Nuneaton line has always been important for the mineral traffic, which still uses the line. The passenger service was withdrawn on 18 January 1965, the same day as for the Leamington line. The Coventry Loop line through Bell Green and Gosford Green, avoiding Coventry station, was opened on 10 August 1914, from Humber Road Jcn on the main line to Three Spires Jcn on the Nuneaton line. The route was 3½ miles long and served factories and industrial concerns — the line was freight only — and closed on 8 April 1972. The Humber Road Jcn to Gosford Green goods section had closed on 7 October 1963. A passenger service was reintroduced between Nuneaton and Coventry from 11 May 1987, and there is a proposal for the Humber Road Jcn to Bell Green line to be converted to a footpath. The intermediate stations have been demolished but there is a fine LNWR signal box with LNWR levers at Hawkesbury Lane. Bedworth station reopened on 16 May 1988.

MONUMENT LANE TO HARBORNE

This short branch, only 4 miles from Birmingham New Street, had three intermediate stations and was opened by the LNWR on 10 August 1874. The Harborne Railway was in fact an independent railway but worked from the onset by the LNWR. There were stations at Icknield Port Road (closed 1931), Rotton Park Road, and Hagley Road. The passenger service was withdrawn on 26 November 1934 but freight lasted well into BR days and ceased on 4 November 1963. The LNWR did not use steam railmotors on the line, probably because of the amount of people using the branch. The line was visited by railtours several times after closure. The trackbed is now a footpath entitled the "Harborne Line Walkway", but the stations have been demolished.

ALDRIDGE TO BROWNHILLS

The Midland Railway Brownhills passenger service commenced on 1 July 1884, the line having opened to freight on 1 April 1882. The line was extended northwards on 1 November 1882, where the Midland was able to tap the lucrative coal traffic from the Cannock Chase collieries who had their own system. Brownhills Midland was not situated too near the town, the LNWR station being better sited. The service was withdrawn on 31 March 1930. There was one intermediate station at Walsall Wood, the 1922 Bradshaw showing only two trains per day — the Midland obviously ran the passenger service as an afterthought. Freight traffic was withdrawn on 1 September 1960 from Brownhills to Walsall Wood, and Walsall Wood to Aldridge on 5 July 1965. The line has since been lifted and the stations demolished.

The section of line around Chasewater Lake is still intact as it is part of the Chasewater Light Railway. The Chasewater Lake is a recreation area sponsored by the local authority and includes sailing, windsurfing, and other associated watersports. The Chasewater Railway is thus well situated to tap the weekend recreation activities of local people. The area is situated between three local authorities: Walsall, West Midlands, and Staffordshire. As a result, the railway has been used as a political football and has, consequently, suffered and not functioned for three years. There have been many hassles as some authorities want the railway and others do not. There is a tale of the track having to be slewed from BR to the NCB to avoid excessive payment.

The motive power consists of several industrial locomotives, a Hawthorn Leslie of 1909 named "Asbestos", an 0-4-0ST, and an 0-4-0ST built by Nielson in 1882 named "Alfred Paget". There are also two Hudswell Clark and Barclay saddle tanks and a Peckett. There is a collection of pre-grouping coaches including six-wheelers and a Maryport and Carlisle Railway carriage of 1879.

The railway society keeps on hoping that the future will be brighter for them and they hope to reopen to day trippers in the summer of 1988. It would be a great pity if the Chasewater Railway failed, as the site is ideal for a small preserved railway. The proposed Northern Relief Road to by-pass the M6 motorway is planned to cut across the site.

HAMPTON-IN-ARDEN TO WHITACRE

A curious piece of railway later owned by the Midland Railway was the line from Hampton-in-Arden to Derby, opened on 12 August 1839 by the Birmingham & Derby Junction Railway. This line was connected with the London & Birmingham at Hampton which opened on 17 September 1838, thus forming the first through route to the North Midlands and Scotland from London. With the construction of other main lines in the 1850s and the opening of Whitacre to Birmingham on 10 February 1842, the line became of little use as a through route. As a branch line the train service had declined to one train per day by 1903 and was eventually withdrawn on 1 January 1917. Freight traffic lasted until 30 April 1939. The line was used for wagon storage until BR days and Coleshill platform can still be seen.

WOLVERHAMPTON TO CASTLE BROMWICH (VIA WALSALL)

The present line from Castle Bromwich Jcn to Walsall, Ryecroft Jcn is still used for freight and the occasional diversion of passenger trains due to engineers' works. At the eastern end of the line there is a spur from Park Lane Jcn to Water Orton West Jcn giving access to the Midland main line to the north. Normal passenger services were withdrawn on 18 January 1965, the service being Birmingham New St to Walsall via Sutton Park. The Midland passenger service from Walsall to Wolverhampton ceased on 5 January 1931. Freight lasted until BR days but the line was closed in connection with the opening of the M6 motorway on 28 September 1964. The Wolverhampton end of the line was used until recently from Wednesfield by Tube Investments. Willenhall to Wednesfield was closed completely on 1 November 1965 — Willenhall to Walsall is to be turned into a footpath.

LICHFIELD CITY TO WALSALL

Opened on 9 April 1849 from Walsall to Wichnor Jcn, the South Staffordshire Railway later became part of the LNWR system with running powers over the Midland to Buxton and Derby. The intermediate stations have been demolished, although Hammerwich station building is now a private house. The passenger service was withdrawn by BR on 18 January 1965 at the same time as the service through to Wolverhampton. The track from Anglesea Sidings, Brownhills LNWR to Walsall (Ryecroft Jcn) was lifted in the autumn of 1986, having closed to freight on 23 January 1984. The line is still used from Anglesea Sidings, Brownhills Charringtons oil terminal to Lichfield and Wichnor Jcn.

RUGELEY TO WALSALL

Opened in 1859, the line passed through the Cannock Chase coalfield and served the collieries of that system which were noted for their antiquated industrial locomotives from obscure builders. The railway is still double track and busy with merry-go-round coal trains passing through serving power stations from the remaining collieries in the area. The line passes through rural countryside from Hednesford to Rugeley.

The line closed to passengers on 18 January 1965 and the stations have been demolished. Cannock and Bloxwich are sizeable towns, the railway is double track and in good condition, but there is no passenger service — a legacy of Beeching thinking. Hednesford (East Cannock Jcn) ceased to be a junction after the line to Norton Crossing Jcn closed to all traffic on 6 January 1964.

BRANCH LINES IN THE BLACK COUNTRY

Walsall today is a branch terminus insofar as the passenger is concerned, but at one time was a junction town of importance, being served by eight different lines. The Midland line to Wolverhampton was cut by the M6 motorway in 1964 and the short remaining piece of line to Birchills power station ceased to be used after 28 September 1964 — the hulk of the power station can still be seen. The once-important Princes End branch from Wednesbury to Tipton lost its passenger service on 1 January 1916 and freight by February 1985. The 3-mile long line is to be turned into a footpath by the local authority.

Walsall to Dudley, although still open for freight, lost its passenger service on 6 July 1964. Dudley to Dudley Port (HL) had a push and pull service which was withdrawn on the same day. The Wednesbury to Darlaston connection had been withdrawn to freight by 1 January 1968.

WELLINGTON TO COALPORT

The 8¼ miles of railway from Hadley to Coalport were opened by the LNWR on 17 June 1861. Part of the branch was constructed over the Shropshire Canal and served an area steeped in industrial history. The LNWR line terminated at Coalport alongside the River Severn. The passenger service provided by the LNWR was fairly sparse and consisted of five trains per day at grouping. The service was withdrawn on 2 June 1952 to passengers and 5 December 1960 to freight. The section from Coalport to Malins Lee is now a footpath called "The Silkin Way". The tunnel under the Blists Hill Museum entrance still exists (now re-graded for the footpath), as does Madeley Market station (now a clinic) and Dawley & Stirchley goods shed.

The Iron Bridge at Coalport across the Severn is of interest as it was built in 1819, and connects the site of the GWR and LNWR stations. The trackbed passes through the new town known as Telford.

WELLINGTON TO STAFFORD

This cross-country line was opened as the Shropshire Union Railway on 1 June 1849, later being acquired by the LNWR. The LNWR treated the line as their through route to Wales, running through coaches not only from Euston to Shrewsbury but also through to Towyn and Aberystwyth on the Welsh coast and to Swansea via Central Wales. Passenger services were withdrawn on 7 September 1964, and freight from Stafford to Newport on 1 August 1966. Newport to Donnington closed to freight on 1 July 1968. The Newport to Stafford section of the line has been converted to a footpath but the line is still open from Wellington to Donnington for the Ordnance Depot. The stations have been demolished on the branch and the site at Newport is now a housing development with the station house being incorporated into it.

CHESTER (TATTENHALL JCN) TO WHITCHURCH

The LNWR ran a through service via this route from Birkenhead to South Wales but the local service was sparse, there being only three stations and a halt. Stations on the route were at Tattenhall, Broxton and Malpas, Malpas station being well over a mile from the town. The line was opened by the LNWR on 1 October 1872 as a double-track main line to rival the Great Western's Shrewsbury to Chester line. The line passed through fine rural Cheshire countryside but with few potential passengers. The branch closed to passengers on 16 September 1957 and freight on 23 March 1964. The line was used for wagon storage for some time after closure. Passenger trains ran on engineering works diversions until 1963. The fate of the three stations on the line has been varied — Tattenhall is now a well restored private house, Broxton has been obliterated and Malpas preserved. The station buildings at Malpas have been well restored by Miles Macadam Surfacing Ltd. The LMS/LMR maroon and cream paintwork has come out well and even the booking hall has been renovated and turned into a reception room for the Company.

OVER & WHARTON

The LNWR opened this mile-long branch on 1 June 1882 which connected with the West Coast main line. The line, which is still open, was built for the salt traffic, and salt is stored in the yard at the old passenger station site. The passenger platform still survives even though the passenger service ceased on 16 June 1947.

NORTHWICH TO SANDBACH

This line was opened for passengers on 1 July 1868, having been opened for freight the previous year. Passenger services ceased on a regular basis on 4 January 1960 and the one remaining intermediate station, at Middlewich, closed. Middlewich station platform edges still survive although the buildings have been demolished. The line is partially single but sees substantial freight traffic and passenger diversions.

RAILWAYS TO BUXTON

The LNWR line from Stockport was opened throughout on 15 June 1863 — the present service is approximately hourly from Manchester Piccadilly and worked by DMMUs. The intermediate stations are well preserved and are at present being refurbished. The present line is the only open passenger line to Buxton, the former Midland lines being used for freight only. The Midland Railway main line via Matlock was opened on 1 June 1863 and terminated next door to the LNWR station. The two stations were side by side and externally identical, the town council insisting upon this. The Midland station has been demolished and the site is being transformed into a by-pass road scheme. The passenger service to the Midland main line was withdrawn by BR on 6 March 1967 to Millers Dale Jcn. The Midland main line service from Matlock to Chinley was withdrawn on 1 July 1968, one of the better known rationalisations of the 1960s era. The LNWR also had a route southwards which was opened in 1899 and included part of the Cromford & High Peak Railway to Ashbourne. The passenger service over this route was withdrawn on 1 November 1954 and most of the line can now be cycled over on the "Tissington Trail" or "High Peak Trail". The stone trains still continue to run from the Hindlow/Dowlow area of the former LNWR line as well as the former Midland line via Peak Forest.

PEAK RAIL BUXTON STEAM CENTRE

Reopening the Midland main line from Buxton to Matlock is the purpose of Peak Rail Ltd who have a steam centre at Buxton alongside the BR station. Most of the main line has been lifted so they have got plenty of work on their plate. The official blurb states that Peak Rail was formed 11 years ago with the object of reopening the 20 miles of railway between Buxton and Matlock. There are problems, such as missing bridges, but if the railway could be reopened it would provide the town with an enormous boost in tourism, as the route over the Peak District to Matlock is highly scenic. At present Darley Dale station has been restored and the sites occupied at Matlock and Buxton — a formidable array of motive power and rolling stock has been gathered together. As a prelude to reopening, Peak Rail have been operating the Peak Rail Rambler on Sundays during the summer from 1985 over the closed BR section from Buxton to Chinley. Starting in 1987, main line steam specials are operating on selected days from Derby and Nottingham via Edale.

Peak Rail possess two class 9, 2-10-0s, an 8F 2-8-0, 0-6-0T 47406, and an "Austerity" 0-6-0ST as well as an extensive collection of industrial tanks and coaches. A lot of restoration work is required on the larger locomotives.

THE LEEK & MANIFOLD VALLEY LIGHT RAILWAY

This was the LMS narrow gauge passenger line of 2′6″ width which ran from Waterhouses to Hulme End and, like that other famous closure of the 1930s, the Lynton & Barnstaple, would be doing very well as a major tourist attraction had it survived into the present age. The Leek & Manifold was just over 8 miles long, ran through superb countryside and was opened on 27 June 1904. Until the standard gauge line reached Waterhouses on 1 July 1905, passenger connection was provided by a NSR steam bus service. The engineer was Mr E.R. Calthrop, who was a consulting engineer specialising in light railways and who had worked in India for several years. The railway was built on his lines and catered for tourists, as well as carrying freight. The LMS closed the line on 12 March 1934 and lifted the track. The LMS donated the trackbed to the Staffordshire County Council who now maintain it as a tarmacadam footpath and cycle-path, except for 2½ miles which is a minor road. The tunnel at Swainsley is part of the road from there to Wetton Mill, and the goods shed at Waterhouses is where bicycles may be hired. E.R. Calthrop was well known for the extensive Barsi Light Railway in India. This Indian railway features many of Calthrop's ideas, and travel over that system, built to the same gauge as the Leek & Manifold, is the best way to sample the real feeling of an English narrow gauge light railway. On three weekends in June, the L&M is revived, as a 10¼″ gauge railway is relaid over part of the course at Hulme End. The trains are hauled by a replica of No 2, "J.B. Earle".

LEEK TO WATERHOUSES

The North Staffordshire Railway opened to Waterhouses on 1 July 1905 with a standard gauge branch from Leek Brook Jcn. The line of 9¾ miles was built to connect with the narrow gauge Leek & Manifold Railway, and Waterhouses was a dual gauge passenger station as well as a transhipment point for goods. Stone trains started to run from Caldon Low Quarry in 1909, this being a branch from the Waterhouses line at Caldon Jcn, 1½ miles short of Waterhouses. The Leek to Waterhouses passenger service ceased on 30 September 1935.

The stone trains to Caldon Low still run, as the quarrying has developed since the original opening and higher tonnages have been extracted following the enlargement of the plant. Today, BR run a regular stone train with extras as required. The original Caldon Low Quarries had an outlet to the canal at Froghall Wharf, the quarries being served by an inclined plane to the canal. The gauge of the quarry system was 3′6″ and although the incline was closed in 1920, the LMS inherited three 3′6″ gauge locomotives from the NSR. The three 0-4-0 saddletanks "Frog", "Toad" and "Bobs" were scrapped on-site in 1936. The stations on the Waterhouses branch have been demolished except Winkhill which is now a house. At Ipstones the railway cottages survive.

THE CHURNET VALLEY RAILWAY (NORTH RODE TO ROCESTER)

In his introduction to "The Churnet Valley Railway", R. Keyes described the railway as "running through some of the most beautiful country in Britain". Well he may be right about the country, but like many railways in fine country it is no longer an operating concern for most of its 23 miles. The Churnet Valley Railway opened on 13 June 1849 and was built as a "main line" linking Manchester to Derby, and became part of the North Stafford until that railway amalgamated into the LMS in 1923. The railway was built over the Trent & Mersey Canal from Froghall to Uttoxeter, the North Stafford Railway having acquired the canal and closed it. The passenger service from North Rode to Leek was withdrawn on 7 November 1960 and from Leek to Uttoxeter on 4 January 1965. Freight traffic ceased from North Rode to Leek on 15 June 1964, and from Oakamoor to Uttoxeter on 4 January 1965. Oakamoor to Leek Brook Jcn and Stoke is still used by BR for sand trains, the section from Leek to Leek Brook having closed completely on 3 July 1970. Leek station has now been demolished although the goods shed survives.

From North Rode to Leek the only surviving station buildings are at Rushton where the station has been well restored and is situated next door to the "Knot Inn". Between Rushton and Leek the course of the line runs alongside Rudyard Lake, an artificial reservoir for the canal which the North Stafford Railway acquired on construction of the line in 1849. As the railway owned the lake and an hotel, the NSR developed the area as a resort for day trippers and provided boating facilities, refreshment stalls and a bandstand. The station site at Rudyard Lake now has a narrow gauge railway which runs to the lake, is 10¼", and the Rudyard Lake Railway (diesel operated) is approximately ½-mile long.

On the Leek to Rocester section the station buildings at Consall, Froghall, Oakamoor and Denistone have been demolished, although platform edges can be seen at Oakamoor, Froghall and Consall. The "pièce de resistance" of the whole line is the station at Alton Towers (originally Alton), which was renovated by the Landmark Trust in 1972 and is used as a holiday letting. The station was built to match the nearby Alton Towers owned by the Earl of Shrewsbury. Oakamoor to Denistone is now the "Churnett Valley Walkway", and Rushton Spencer to Leek the "Churnet Valley Footpath". Cheddleton station is now preserved by the North Staffordshire Railway Centre. The station buildings have been repainted in chocolate and cream. At the station is an interesting museum of NSR relics and the booking hall has a rare photograph of George Stephenson and Brunel which is an original. The North Staffordshire Railway Centre has a good collection of locomotives and rolling stock and runs trains on a short stretch of line adjacent to the BR tracks. A new loco shed contains a 4F 0-6-0 (44422), 4MT 2-6-4 (80136) and a 0-6-0 Hunslet "Austerity" of 1952. There is also an 08 class DSL, a NSR signalbox and coach body, and a promise of NSR No 2, 0-6-2 T now at Chatterly Whitfield.

The North Staffordshire Railway Centre is open on Sundays from April to September, including Bank Holiday weekends. The Centre would also like to have the four-wheeled battery electric locomotive built at Stoke in 1917 which was used for shunting at Oakamoor and is restored in NSR livery. The locomotive is at present in the National Collection.

ASHBOURNE TO UTTOXETER

The NSR opened the Ashbourne branch on 31 May 1852, the Rocester to Uttoxeter section having been opened on 13 July 1849 as part of the Churnet Valley Railway. There were two intermediate stations at Norbury and Clifton. Both of these survive as private dwellings. The NSR had a monopoly on Ashbourne until the LNWR appeared on the scene in 1899 with an extension from Buxton and the High Peak. The LNWR ran a through service to Euston to rival the Midland, via Ashbourne and Nuneaton until 1916. Rocester to Ashbourne closed to passengers on 1 November 1954 and goods on 1 June 1964. Rocester today has been built over by a factory but the goods shed survives as a club house. Norbury station is well restored complete with traders stores. Clifton is being restored by Mr & Mrs Birkinshaw, and what a job they have got! Ashbourne station site is a car park, but the goods shed remains. The "Tissington Trail" starts at the north end of the, now fenced off, Ashbourne tunnel.

BURTON TO TUTBURY

An outpost of the Knotty was the line into Burton-on-Trent from Tutbury, the NSR main line being the direct route to Derby. Burton to Tutbury, a distance of 5½ miles, was opened on 11 September 1848, being part of the route from Uttoxeter. The line became worked by a push and pull unit and ceased to function as such when the passenger service was withdrawn by BR on 13 June 1960. Freight trains ceased to run after 6 May 1968. The "Tutbury Jenny" — as the service was known — served three intermediate stations at Horninglow, Stretton and Clay Mills, and Rolleston-on-Dove. The rotting remains of Horninglow can still be seen.

CRESSWELL TO CHEADLE

The Cheadle Railway opened on 1 January 1901, was nearly 4 miles long and worked by the North Stafford. There was one intermediate station at Tean, the NSR providing substantial buildings at both stations, which have since been demolished. The line was built to serve collieries in the area and was famous for the tunnel which kept giving way. In 1918 the brick lining gave way and after several patch-ups the LMS decided to build a diversion around the tunnel. This diversion opened on 26 November 1933. The branch always had a sparse passenger service under the LMS and BR, and when it was closed on 17 June 1963 only had two passenger trains per day. The sand trains from Cheadle ran until recently and the track on the branch is still in position, although the junction at Cresswell was severed in 1985. The public freight use of the line ceased on 6 March 1978 with only the civil engineer using the line afterwards.

BRANCH LINES IN THE POTTERIES
The Potteries' loop line from Etruria Jcn to Kidsgrove was completed on 15 November 1875 including Tunstall to Longport, which was opened to goods on 1 June 1875. The loop line served many industrial installations and collieries in the expanding area to the east of Stoke and an intensive passenger service developed under NSR auspices. In 1908, the peak year, the loop line carried 3,000,000 passengers. Tunstall to Longport Jcn closed on 17 February 1964 to all traffic. The Kidsgrove to Etruria passenger service was withdrawn on 2 March 1964. The same day also saw the Stoke to Silverdale passenger service withdrawn. The whole of the loop line had been closed back to Etruria from Kidsgrove by 4 August 1969. Most of the trackbed is now a footpath and cycle-path known as the "Potteries Greenway" and "Greenway Link", with the station buildings demolished. The buildings at Waterloo Road are still in existence on the road overbridge. There were many mineral lines in the area, some Knotty owned, some privately. A brief mention of the principal mineral branches closed is appended; Jamage 21 December 1947, Newfields 3 August 1959, Grange 29 October 1961, Pool Dam 7 October 1967, and Chesterton 21 June 1968.

STOKE-ON-TRENT TO MARKET DRAYTON
Silverdale to Market Drayton opened for both passenger and goods traffic on 1 February 1870, giving connection between the NSR system and the Great Western's Nantwich to Wellington line. The NSR ran a frequent passenger service to Silverdale but beyond Keele the line ran through sparsely populated countryside. Passenger services were withdrawn from Market Drayton to Silverdale on 7 May 1956 and Silverdale to Stoke on 2 March 1964. The line is still used from Madeley Road to Silverdale and Holditch Colliery via Madeley Chord Jcn. The Madeley Chord was laid anew by BR on a hitherto unused formation. BR lifted the line to Market Drayton after freight ceased running on 1 May 1967 on the Nantwich to Wellington line. The section from Apedale Jcn was lifted after cessation of freight from there to Stoke on 1 June 1970.

The station at Silverdale is complete, even though the regular passenger service ceased in 1964. Newcastle-under-Lyme station is now a scrapyard but Keele station house is well preserved as a private residence — there is a NSR "knot" and the date "1871" is inscribed in the wall of the house. The other stations on the line have been demolished but Madeley Road still has a platform for crew changes — a very isolated spot.

KEELE TO ALSAGER JUNCTION
The line from Alsager Jcn to Keele was opened for goods on 24 July 1870 and was built to serve the coal mines in the area, of which there were a considerable number. The area was one of the richest coal-mining areas in Britain, with many privately owned colliery railway systems, most of which are now closed — the mines having been worked out. The passenger service introduced on 26 June 1880 lasted until 27 April 1931 when the LMS had a purge nationwide. The freight traffic lasted until 18 June 1962 on the Audley to Keele section and 7 January 1963 on the Audley to Alsager section. Most of the line today has disappeared and the station sites built over. At Halmer End on the site of the station, a walk commences along the old trackbed to Audley. The housing development is situated appropriately in "Station Walks".

SANDBACH TO LAWTON JUNCTION (WHEELOCK)
The section of line from Lawton Jcn to Wheelock opened to goods on 21 January 1852 but the connection through to Sandbach on the Manchester (LNWR) main line was not completed until 1866. The LNWR did not encourage through working, and the NSR service to passengers introduced on 3 July 1893 only ran from Harecastle to Wheelock — a distance of 6¼ miles. The LMS withdrew the passenger service on 28 July 1930 as part of the economies effected during that period. Today, although the line has been lifted, the station at Hassall Green is complete and can be seen from the nearby M6 motorway. The station buildings at Wheelock at street level are complete at present and are a remarkable survival, having been used as the "Battery Service Station" until recently. The proprietor has retired after 40 years, so the buildings — which are of timber — may not last. The station buildings still have a driveway from the main road and the rear of the old booking hall is still in LMS brown paintwork. The line had ceased to operate back to Lawton Jcn by 4 January 1971. A short walk runs along the trackbed from Wheelock station to the golf course.

STOKE TO CONGLETON (VIA BIDDULPH)
Stoke to Congleton (Upper Jcn) and Brunswick Goods opened on 28 August 1860, passenger services being introduced from Stoke to Congleton on 1 June 1864 and withdrawn by the LMS on 11 July 1927. BR closed Heaths Jcn to Congleton Lower on 1 April 1968 — the connection to the main line having been closed to all traffic on 1 December 1963. The last section back to Milton Jcn from Ford Green (Norton Colliery) ceased to be used after 24 June 1972. Staffordshire County Council have

made good use of the trackbed and opened a footpath from Biddulph to Congleton Brunswick (Ches) with plans to extend southwards to Heaths Jcn (Fegg Hayes). The walk is to be known as the "Stoke City Greenway", over which freight services ceased to run after 17 April 1976 (Ford Green–Chatterley Whitfield).

Of the stations on the line, Biddulph has been tastefully restored as a private house, but the rest have been demolished. Chatterley Whitfield is where the mining museum has been set up — of interest to railway enthusiasts is the collection of private colliery wagons. The museum also houses the last Knotty steam locomotive to exist — 0-6-2T No 2, built at Stoke in 1923.

STOKE TO LEEK
Milton Jcn to Cheddleton Jcn opened to passengers and freight on 1 November 1867, giving a direct service between Leek and Stoke. The Churnet Valley had already arrived on the scene nearly 20 years earlier in July 1849. The passenger service was withdrawn on 7 May 1956 but the line remains in use as Caldon Low stone and Oakamoor sand travel this way via Leek Brook Jcn. Of the stations on the line, Wall Grange has been demolished but Endon platform has survived with LMS green and cream paint on the fences. Stockton Brook station buildings survive at street level as a newsagents known as "Station News". The line has been singled and at Milton and Bucknall the buildings have been demolished although the platforms still remain.

TRENTHAM GARDENS (PARK)
This was the last passenger line opened by the Knotty, being 1 mile 14 chains in length and opened on 1 April 1910 to serve Trentham Gardens on the outskirts of Stoke. The line was built to take visitors to Trentham Hall, the former home of the Duke of Sutherland. The NSR ran a railmotor service for commuters until 1919, there being an intermediate halt at Hanford Road. A feature of this short line was the station at Trentham Jcn which was connected to Trentham on the main line. Trentham station is of architectural significance, having been designed by Sir Charles Barry for the Duke of Sutherland. The building is still in existence as a bank. Trentham Gardens, renamed Trentham Park by the LMS on 7 October 1946, was going to be extended to Pool Dam to provide an avoiding line to Stoke, but the scheme was not taken up. The earthworks and a bridge over the main road outside Trentham Park were constructed, but the bridge was demolished in the Second World War. Astute observers will notice some brickwork still in position across the road from the station site which has now been built upon. The line was closed by BR on 1 October 1957 — it was used only by excursions from 1939, the last one having run on 25 August 1957.

COLD MEECE
This line was built during World War Two to serve an ordnance factory and opened in 1941. The branch left the main line at Swynnerton Jcn, between Norton Bridge and Stone, and was served by workmen's trains from the Potteries area. The line opened on 5 August 1941 and lasted until 1958 under BR. The line had a passenger service only and this ceased on 27 June 1958. The branch never appeared in a timetable or even on a map. The line was approximately 1½ miles long and was used for stabling empty coaching stock until 1960 on Wakes Saturdays. The terminus consisted of four platforms, all in concrete. The station site is now occupied by a goods vehicle testing station. Munitions trains served the depot from a siding on the West Coast main line.

Over & Wharton terminus as seen in 1987 and still in use. This former LNWR line from Winsford Jcn had a passenger service of five trains per day from Hartford (on weekdays only) when the LMS was formed in 1923. The LMS withdrew the passenger service from 16 June 1947 but BR still use the line to store wagons and to serve the ICI saltworks.

Wheelock is a remarkable survival, as the station buildings still exist even though the line which the station served closed to passengers as long ago as 28 July 1930. The station is still in LMS colours at the rear, a dingy brown applied to LMS goods buildings and warehouses. The platform site is now a public footpath to the nearby golf course.

The Trentham Gardens branch with a "crab" 2-6-0 and lengthy train during BR days. The line ceased to have a regular service from 1927 and the LMS only ran specials and excursions until 1948. The last advertised passenger train was on 25 August 1957, BR having run excursions on occasions from 1948. Photo by C.H.A. Townley.

Trentham, on the main line, had a branch platform on the Trentham Gardens branch which was known as Trentham Junction. The branch platform and main station were connected by a footpath. The station building designed in 1848 by Sir Charles Barry of House of Commons fame still exists and has been converted into a bank. Photograph taken in 1950 by Real Photos.

North Staffordshire branch lines featured here include Rushton (left) on 3 June 1960 with a class 4, 2-6-4T, and Leek (top) on the same day. Rushton still survives as a private house and Leek has been demolished. The Churnet Valley line was one of Britain's most picturesque branches and closed to passengers from North Rode to Leek on 7 November 1960, and Leek to Uttoxeter on 4 January 1965. The scene below depicts a North Staffs 0-6-4 tank at Waterhouses in LMS days with Midland stock. Photograph by Brookside.
An annual event not known outside the area is the re-creation of the Leek & Manifold Railway in June on a 10¼" gauge replica line at Hulme End laid on the old track bed.

Rushton

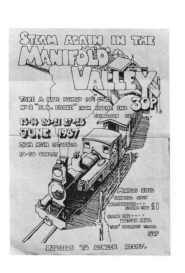

Cheadle, in BR days, with BR class 4, 2-6-4T No 42593 on 25 July 1961 when the line only had two trains per day, one in the morning, and one in the afternoon. There was a Saturday train to Llandudno during the summer only. This outpost of the former North Staffordshire Railway not surprisingly had few customers, only the occasional gricer.

Cheadle, as it is today — the spacious buildings have been demolished but the platform and loading dock for engineers mineral trains still remain. No trains have run on the branch in recent years but it is still not officially closed — an unusual arrangement for a BR owned line. The sparse passenger service ceased on 17 June 1963.

Tean was the intermediate station on the Cheadle branch, seen here in pre-war days. The platform has milk churns, North Staffs Railway seats and enamel sign boards. The chocolate machine, once a common feature on British stations, disappeared during World War 2 when confectionery became rationed. The Cheadle branch was well known for its tunnel which collapsed and the subsequent deviation built around it. Photo by Lens of Sutton.

Camp Hill on 1 June 1954 with LNWR 0-6-2T No 58903 taking water with an SLS Railtour of the West Midlands. The station buildings have survived in this picture although the platforms have been demolished as the service was withdrawn on 27 January 1941 to passengers. The line is still in use for through trains. The LNWR "Coal Tanks" introduced from 1881 and consisting of 300 engines, never had smokebox number plates fitted under BR as the metal used was too soft and would cause a burn through the smokebox door. Photo: N. Glover.

The Harborne branch was an early LNWR suburban line from New St. In this photograph a "Coal Tank" is seen shunting the sidings in LMS days. The line closed to passengers on 22 November 1934 and freight on 4 November 1963. The trackbed is now a footpath. Photograph by Lens of Sutton.

Before and after at Dunchurch — class 2-6-2T No 41227 on the Leamington to Rugby branch in 1959 prior to closure (upper). The platforms have become overgrown and the track awaits removal in the view below.

Hard times at Birdingbury — the photograph (above) shows the branch push & pull with 41227 on 4 April 1959. The photograph (below) shows the same station in 1986; the track has now been removed.

Coalport, with pre-Grouping stock (probably LNWR) and summer foliage. The station was the terminus of the short branch from Hadle and closed on 2 June 1952 to passengers. A feature at Coalport was the combined carriage and engine shed. Part of the line is now a pu footpath. Photo: Lens of Sutton.

Aldridge on 26 May 1951 with class 2, 2-6-2 T No 41226 on an SLS special to Brownhills. The leading vehicle of the "sandwich" is a LNWR push and pull coach. Photo by N. Glover.

Knapton & Stockton station on the Weedon to Leamington branch closed on 15 September 1958. The station was a typical LNWR wooden building of the early years of the century. Graham and Peter Lockley with their mother and sister admire the passing train.

The Birmingham & Derby Junction Railway opened from Hampton-in-Arden to Derby in 1839 and became a main line, but when alternative routes opened the section from Whitacre to Hampton became a branch. There was one intermediate station at Coleshill (renamed Maxstoke in 1923), and this was served by passenger trains until 1917. The platform still survives, very much overgrown, although the buildings have been demolished. Photo by Lens of Sutton.

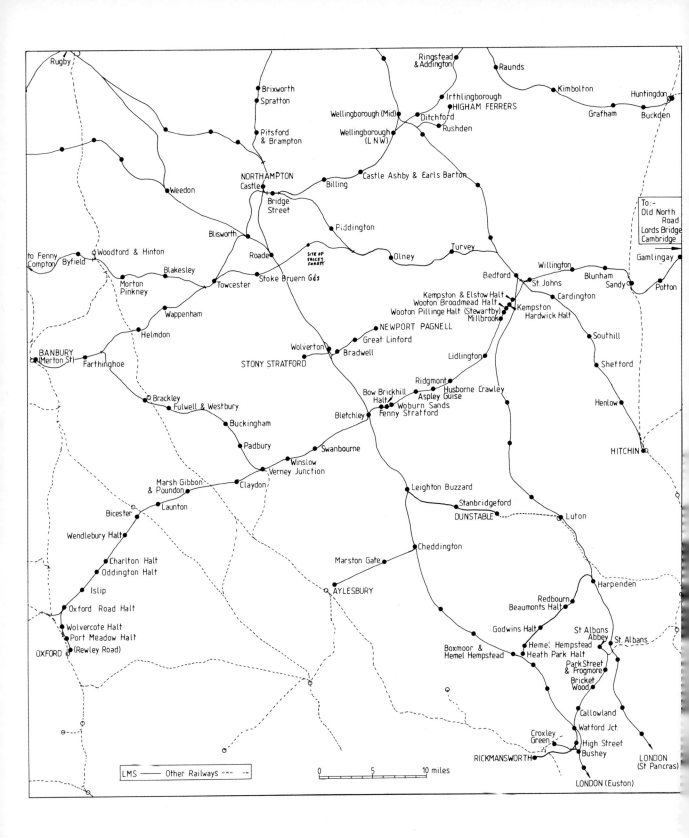

REDDITCH TO ASHCHURCH

The Birmingham & Gloucester Railway opened up for business on 17 December 1840, the terminus being at Camp Hill. The B&G promotors were so keen to get the line going that they had the line constructed as direct as possible and this resulted in the 1 in 37¾ Lickey incline. Lickey was and still is one of the steepest parts of the main line system. The need for an alternative route via Redditch was sponsored by the Midland and the first section of line from Barnt Green to Redditch opened to passengers on 19 September 1859. The Ashchurch to Evesham section opened on 1 October 1864, and the section from Evesham to Redditch by 4 May 1868. Barnt Green to Ashchurch was worked by the Midland Railway over the 32½ mile length. Connection was made with the GWR at Alcester, and Evesham (where the Midland station was alongside the GWR) and the Stratford-upon-Avon & Midland Jcn at Broom.

The passenger service between Redditch and Ashchurch was withdrawn on 17 June 1963, Evesham to Alcester closing to all traffic on the same date. A bus service operated between Evesham and Redditch from 1 October 1962 due to the state of the track. Freight services between Ashchurch and Evesham ceased on 9 September 1963 and between Alcester and Redditch on 6 July 1964. Redditch (relocated on 7 February 1972) remains open with a fairly frequent service to Birmingham New Street throughout the day.

Today, the section of the line from Wixford to Broom and Salford Priors is partly a footpath. Most stations still exist and have been converted into private residences. Ashchurch has been demolished, but Beckford, Ashton and Hinton are now private houses. Bengeworth site is now occupied by a housing estate, Evesham (Midland) buildings still exist, and Harvington is now a private house. Salford Priors is an office and Broom a council salt store — but the buildings survive. Wixford platform still survives and at Alcester the station house is still used but the goods yard is an industrial estate. At Coughton Mr Braithwaite and his wife have taken up residence and restored the station, where an enamel nameboard still survives with white lettering on a blue background — this was the Midland standard. Studley & Astwood Bank station is a nice little country station that has survived complete with LMS dark brown paintwork on the goods shed doors.

ASHCHURCH TO UPTON-ON-SEVERN

Ashchurch station was unusual in that it had platforms serving three lines and a flat level crossing with direct running from Evesham to the Tewkesbury line across the main line. This endearing LMS branch was originally a through line from Great Malvern to Ashchurch, a distance of 14 miles with four trains per day throughout in 1922. Under BR, the stretch from Malvern Wells (Malvern Jcn) to Upton-on-Severn closed to all traffic on 1 December 1952. Passenger services from Upton-on-Severn to Ashchurch ceased on 14 August 1961, and freight on 1 July 1963, despite provision of a new bridge and ¼ mile of approach diversion line over the M50 motorway, back to Tewkesbury. The Tewkesbury to Ashchurch section finally closed to freight on 2 November 1964. The line in its final form only had two passenger trains per day but was a haven for old Midland locomotive types until displaced by GWR pannier tanks.

The line today has been demolished and Malvern Wells, Upton-on-Severn and Tewkesbury stations have disappeared, but there is one gem that is worthy of a visit. Ripple station has recently been purchased and its owner, Val Fullerlove, has restored the building to its original state with a few improvements. Flowers, plants and shrubs adorn the station, platforms and trackbed — a visit to this well restored station is recommended especially in the summer when the flowers are in full bloom.

COALEY TO DURSLEY

This 2½ mile branch had seven trains a day in Midland days, calling at an intermediate station at Cam. Little remains to be seen today as Cam has been demolished and only the platform edges exist. The site of Dursley station is now occupied by a car park. The passenger service was withdrawn on 10 September 1962, and freight on 13 July 1970. The line was worked by class 1F Midland 0-6-0Ts with half cab in early BR days. The Midland tanks were later replaced by GWR pannier tanks.

YATE TO THORNBURY

This 7½ mile line had an infrequent service in Midland days, there being only three trains per day, two of which ran through to Bristol. There were two intermediate stations at Iron Acton and Tytherington. The line was opened on 2 September 1872 and passenger services lasted until 19 June 1944. The line is still used to Tytherington Quarry at Grovesend where railway ballast is extracted. The Thornbury line closed to freight on 3 September 1967 from Yate and the track was lifted. Yate to Tytherington Quarry reopened on 3 July 1972 to convey the stone to the main line. Relaying the line involved building a new level crossing over the Iron Acton by-pass, which road had been built during the period of total closure. Yate station on the main Bristol to Gloucester line has lost its platforms but the station house and goods shed in a fine Gothic style survive. Negotiations currently continue over the possible reopening of Yate station for passengers. At Iron Acton the platform has been demolished but the station house is still used. Tytherington was a nice country station but, although the approach path is now overgrown, is still intact. Thornbury station has been demolished and an industrial estate occupies the site, Midland Way, commemorating the station.

STROUD & NAILSWORTH

The Midland operated a branch line with six passenger trains a day to Nailsworth (5¾ miles), from which there was a short line (1 mile) into Stroud (Cheapside) station, situated about ¼ mile from the main GWR station in Russell Street. Both lines succumbed to local bus competition, closing to passengers on 16 June 1947, the official date under BR ownership being 8 June 1949. Goods trains continued under BR until 1 June 1966. The Nailsworth branch is now a footpath and the terminal station is well preserved as a private house. The goods warehouse and "Station Hotel" survive today. The wooden station building at Stroud (renamed Wallbridge under BR) was in use until recently as a store but has now been demolished.

THE STRATFORD-UPON-AVON & MIDLAND JUNCTION RAILWAY

The Stratford-upon-Avon & Midland Junction Railway, as it latterly became known, was a minor constituent of the LMS. It consisted of a "main line" of 55½ miles, a 4¼ mile branch from Towcester to Blisworth and a 16½ mile line from Towcester to Banbury, the last 5½ miles, over which SMJ trains had running powers, being over the LNWR Buckingham to Banbury branch.

The railway had a shoestring existence throughout its working life as it passed through rural parts of the country with no large towns on its route apart from Stratford.

The first section of the system to be opened was from Blisworth to Towcester on 1 May 1866, followed by Towcester to Cockley Brake Jcn on 1 June 1872 as the Northampton & Banbury Junction Railway. Towcester to Stratford opened on 1 July 1873 and the extension on to Broom Jcn on 2 June 1879 — this line became known as the East & West Junction Railway. The final section to be opened was from Towcester to Ravenstone Wood Jcn on 13 April 1891 where the line joined the Midland Railway's Northampton to Bedford branch. The SMJ was formed in 1910 by amalgamation of the E&WJR and the N&BJR and lasted as such until grouped into the LMS in 1923.

Traffic on the line was light, the other main line railways mostly preferring their own routes. Heavy through traffic did not materialise until after nationalisation. This occurred especially when BR put in connections ast Fenny Compton and Stratford in 1960 to run freight trains off the GWR main line to South Wales via Stratford and Honeybourne. Passenger trains were sparse, there being three trains a day on the "main line" and only two on the Banbury branch during the last year of operation by the SMJ in the summer of 1922. A through service from Stratford to Marylebone was implemented by the Great Central when the GCR arrived on the scene. This was the shortest route to London and ran via Byfield and Woodford, for which the GCR provided a through coach. The SMJ passenger service did not last for very long after the nationalisation of the LMS in 1948 as all passenger services were withdrawn after 7 April 1952. The Stratford to Broom section was closed to passengers by the LMS from 16 June 1947 and the Towcester to Banbury branch by BR on 2 July 1951. A curious feature of the SMJ was the line from Towcester to Ravenstone Wood Jcn which only had a passenger service from Towcester to Olney from December 1892 to March 1893. Under BR the system had a new lease of life in the 1960s but eventually the freight traffic was diverted to other routes and the "main line" had closed to all traffic by 5 July 1965, the Stratford to Broom section having closed to freight on 13 June 1960. Blisworth to Towcester closed to freight from 3 February 1964, the section of the N&BJ from Towcester to Cockley Brake Jcn having closed to all traffic on 29 October 1951. There was a railtour organised by the SLS on 14 May 1960 which traversed the connection at Fenny Compton from the GWR main line and also the connection at Stratford onto the GWR Honeybourne line. The train used the Stratford to Broom section and was probably the only passenger train to traverse the "new" BR connections. The railtour was the last train from Stratford to Broom Jcn.

The Towcester to Ravenstone Wood Jcn section closed officially on 30 June 1958, although the exact running of the last train is not certain as the line was used to store wagons. Contrary to popular belief the line was not obliterated to make way for the M1 motorway, as the motorway bridged it near Salcey Forest. The trackbed can still be seen from the M1 and the bridge over the railway site is still in situ.

THE LINE TODAY

The SMJ is a very mysterious railway to today's generation of railway fans, as it was closed to passengers many years ago and since then parts of the railway trackbed have been ploughed back into fields by local farmers. The train service was limited and intermediate stations difficult to reach, so relatively few photographs survive. The best preserved station is one of the two that closed in 1893 and is currently being renovated for conversion to a private house. Broom Jcn is used by the local authority as a road salt store and the buildings still exist. Bidford-on-Avon is built upon and is now a factory; Binton is still in existence, used by a contractor. The goods shed survives with the LMS faded green and cream paintwork still being visible. Stratford-on-Avon is now demolished and the site awaits development as a new road. Beyond Stratford the course of the railway through the 60ft deep Goldicote cutting can be easily discerned from the main road. Ettington station still exists, having been converted into a private house and is part of a farm. The goods shed is also in existence and still shows the LMS paintwork. Kineton station has been built upon, the site now being an industrial estate. The only part of the former SMJ still in use is the line from Kineton Ordnance depot to Fenny Compton. This section was sold by BR to the Ministry of Defence in 1971. Little remains of the SMJ platforms at Fenny Compton whilst Byfield, Moreton Pinkney, Blakesley and Towcester have been completely demolished. Towcester station site is now occupied by an engineering company who make tubes. Blakesley station had a narrow gauge railway running to Blakesley Hall, both now demolished.

On the Towcester to Ravenstone Wood line, Stoke Bruerne station survives in good condition having been converted into a private dwelling recently. This is a remarkable survival considering that passenger services were withdrawn in 1893. The interior of Stoke Bruerne station was painted dark red lower, black line and green upper, the exterior being painted brown and maroon — this could be the SMJ station livery. There is no connection with the nearby canal, village or tunnel. On the Banbury line, Wappenham station has been demolished but the platform edge survives. Helmdon is now a garage for Jeff's Coaches and the station building has been converted into a private house.

BANBURY TO VERNEY JUNCTION

The LNWR had a branch of 21¼ miles from Verney Jcn, on the cross-country Bletchley–Oxford line, to its own terminus at Banbury, entitled "Merton Street", across the road from the GWR station. The railway could be described as a typical country branch line, the principal intermediate station being at Buckingham. The line was opened on 1 May 1850 as the Buckinghamshire Railway, a satellite of the LNWR. The section from Banbury to Buckingham was used by BR in August 1956 for an experiment using single unit railcars, tickets issued on the train and two new halts at Radclive and Water Stratford. The railcar experiment did not last for long, as passenger services were withdrawn on 2 January 1961 from Banbury to Buckingham, with the section onto Verney Jcn following on 7 September 1964. Freight trains ceased to run on 2 December 1963 between Banbury and Buckingham, and Buckingham to Verney Jcn on 5 December 1966.

The unusual wooden terminus of the LNWR at Merton Street, Banbury, has now been demolished, the track being lifted in 1967. Farthinghoe, an idyllic, wooden LNWR station, has been demolished and is now a council rubbish tip. Brackley station has been razed to the ground, with only the pub opposite the station as a reminder of the former branch. The pub is aptly named "The Locomotive" and has a picture of an LNWR "Jumbo" on the inn sign. At Fulwell & Westbury the station platform remains but is devoid of buildings. The crossing keeper's house also remains. Buckingham station is now completely demolished and Padbury is a housing estate, "Station Road" commemorating the railway.

BLETCHLEY TO BEDFORD

Part of the LNWR "Oxbridge" line which was 77¼ miles long consisted of the Bedford Railway which was the first section to be opened on 17 November 1846. The London & Birmingham Railway management had proposed a branch from Bletchley to Bedford in 1844 but by the time the line was completed, the L&BR had become part of the LNWR. The line is still in use today and has some interesting relics dating from pre-LMS days. The stations on the Bletchley to Bedford line were constructed in an architectural style known as "Half Timbered Gothic" — this was at the insistence of the Duke of Bedford whose estates the line traversed. The Gothic timbered buildings still exist although some of them are in a very poor state of repair. In addition to the conventional stations along the Bedford Railway, the LNWR introduced a steam railmotor service in December 1905, opening seven new halts. Some of these were closed in 1926, and the picturesquely-named Husborne Crawley, Wootton Pillinge, Wootton Broadmead, and Kempston & Elstow halts are now but a memory. Bow Brickhill, Aspley Guise, and Kempston Hardwick, survive today, being served by the BR Bedford Midland to Bletchley DMU service, an outpost of Network South East.

Ridgmont station has an LNWR open frame on the platform and is a one-man operated station. At Lidlington, the next station towards Bedford, there is also an LNWR open frame. The Lidlington frame is claimed to be a unique survival as the keys interlock into the crossing gates from the frame. At Millbrook the station building has been sold and is being renovated. There is another LNWR open frame here and wooden steps for passengers, as the platforms are low for modern stock. This once-common LMS/LNWR feature is now fairly rare. The crossing gates at Kempston Hardwick are now fully automatic and the station unstaffed. At Bedford the former LNWR station of St Johns is closed, the present halt having been built on the existing connection onto the former Midland main line. The layout at Bedford has been modified in recent years, the former LNWR line through the town having crossed the Midland Bedford to Hitchin branch on the level. Bedford St Johns LNWR station closed to all traffic on 14 May 1984, trains now running to the Midland station. A new halt by Ampthill Road bridge has been provided, entitled "Bedford St Johns". Several attempts have been made to close the line to Bletchley but with the expansion of Milton Keynes the traffic potential has increased.

BEDFORD TO CAMBRIDGE

The first section of the Bedford to Cambridge line to be opened was that of the Sandy & Potton Railway on 25 June 1857, a distance of 3½ miles. this local railway was the protégé of Captain William Peel, son of the former prime minister. A curious survival of this railway is the 0-4-0 well tank "Shannon" built in 1857 for the line's opening and now kept by the Great Western

Society at Didcot. The locomotive, built by George England & Co of Hatcham (an area of London near Old Kent Road) is still steamed occasionally by the Great Western Society, and is one of the oldest usable steam locomotives in existence. The engine shed that housed "Shannon" still exists at Potton.

Bedford through to Cambridge was opened for passenger traffic on 7 July 1862 as the Bedford & Cambridge Railway, which became part of the LNWR in July 1865. The railway incorporated the Sandy & Potton as well as crossing the East Coast Main Line at Sandy on a skew bridge. The B&C had its own station side by side with the GNR at Sandy.

Stations on the Bedford to Cambridge section were of a distinctive style architecturally, with yellow brickwork, and most still exist. The stations were built to a common theme but each building had a slight variation, as can be seen today (most of the buildings survive now as private houses or offices). The architecture was individual to the line only and not typical of the LNWR. The only station built in timber was Willington, opened in 1903 and of all-timber LNWR standard design. The section of the line from Bedford to Sandy was originally single track with passing loops at the stations. The line closed to all traffic on 1 January 1968 and was lifted shortly afterwards. The only pieces of line which survived after that date were (a) the section from Bedford St Johns to Goldington Power Station which was lifted in 1981, and (b) Long Headshunt at Cambridge on the LNWR formation.

Of the intermediate stations, nothing can be seen today of Willington but the others, in the substantial Bedford & Cambridge Railway yellow brick, remain. Blunham is in a good state of repair and is in use as an office with the wooden platform shelter still in situ. Potton has been restored by Mr Howe, a local railway enthusiast, historian, and BR employee. Gamlingay is neatly restored and in good condition. At Old North Road, David Jackson has restored the building and lives in it; he also uses the goods shed to run his engineering business. The signalbox and waiting shelter are still in existence, still in fading BR(E) green and cream colours. Lords Bridge is now the Mullard Radio Astronomy Observatory lecture room, the station being in a good state of repair.

BLETCHLEY TO OXFORD

The section of line from Bletchley to Oxford was opened by the LNWR in 1851 and is still in use for freight, diversionary, and empty stock working. The LNWR had its own terminus at Oxford named Rewley Road. This closed on 4 October 1951, on passenger services being directed to Oxford (GWR). The frontage at Rewley Road is still there, being used as a motor exhaust centre. The LNWR inaugurated a steam railmotor service between Bicester and Oxford on 9 October 1905, which lasted until 25 October 1926 and included rail-level halts. Recently the line has reopened to passengers, courtesy of BR, Network South East, and a passenger service commenced on 11 May 1987. The passenger service from Oxford to Bletchley was withdrawn by BR on 1 January 1968.

The Bletchley to Oxford line today has been singled for most of the way but a few interesting survivals can still be seen. At Swanbourne the station is virtually unchanged with two levels of platform. Fred Walter, the late resident, carved a fine piece of topiary out of the hedge which depicts an LNWR 0-8-0, class G2 — this can still be seen. The booking office retains the LMS green and cream paintwork while the former goods yard has the LNWR lamp hut, complete with number — a rare survival on a station that closed in 1968. At Winslow the station is also complete but in a very poor state of repair. The building is partly in LMS green and cream and LMR maroon and cream colours. Of the other stations on this line, Verney Jcn, Claydon, and Marsh Gibbon & Pounden still have their platform edges, Launton has an automatic crossing barrier and Islip still retains it station house though the station itself has been demolished. Oxford to Cambridge had an early diesel multiple unit service the LMS introduced in 1938 which took 1¾ hours to cover the 77¼ miles. Built by Leyland, the multiple unit was somewhat similar to vehicles in use on the Great Northern of Ireland until the 1960s.

BEDFORD TO HITCHIN

This was the main line of the Midland Railway prior to the opening of the route to St Pancras. After the direct route opened, Bedford to Hitchin became a cross-country branch line of little importance. The Midland Railway had originally intended to link up with the Eastern Counties Railway at Hertford and run over the ECR to London, but the Midland was thwarted by its rivals and trains had to run by the GNR from Hitchin to Kings Cross until the Midland opened its own main line in 1868 to St Pancras. Bedford to Hitchin was linked by rail in 8 May 1857 and opened as a double track line. BR closed the line to passengers on 1 January 1962. Freight closures were: Bedford to Cardington on 29 April 1969, Cardington to Shefford on 28 December 1964, and Shefford to Hitchin on 30 December 1963.

The line today has some interesting survivals of the past. Henlow Camp station, the first one from Hitchin, has been built over and the site is now occupied by the local post office. Shefford is now a housing estate but Southill has been well restored as a private residence. An excellent restoration, Southill still has a Midland Railwaya lamp store with an "×" scissors shape on the brickwork. Cardington station buildings still exist and show signs of LMS green and cream paint on the timberwork. The premises are used for a scrap motorcar business, while the famous RAF airship sheds nearby are still used by Airship Industries Ltd.

BEDFORD TO NORTHAMPTON

This branch was opened on 10 June 1872, and worked by the Midland Railway to its own terminus at Northampton St. Johns Street. The station was situated near Bridge Street and closed on 3 July 1939. The Bedford passenger trains were diverted to Castle station by using the reversed connection between the MR and LNWR lines newly installed by the LMS after that date. The line was dieselised in 1958 but closed to passengers on 5 March 1962. Goods traffic ceased on 20 January 1964 apart from the military depot at Piddington which was connected by rail to Northampton (Hardingstone Jcn) until the summer of 1987 when track lifting commenced, about three years after closure. From Piddington to Bedford the track was removed in 1965 and little remains of the fine county stations at Turvey and Olney. Piddington station remains, devoid of platforms and inhabited by a retired railway man.

The Bedford to Northampton line was connected at Ravenstonewood Junction (between Olney and Piddington) with the ill-fated Stratford-on-Avon, Midland & Towcester Junction Railway. The line which became part of the SMJ was little used by passenger trains but was useful to the Midland who ran freight, parcels, and empty stock trains from the main line at Bedford across to Broom Jcn and their West of England main line.

WOLVERTON TO NEWPORT PAGNELL

The 4-mile branch from Wolverton to Newport Pagnell could be described as a true branch line in the traditional sense, being single track throughout and serving local needs. The LNWR opened the Newport Pagnell branch on 2 September 1867. There were two intermediate stations at Great Linford and Bradwell. The service consisted of seven trains per day each way and was push and pull worked by an ex-LMS class 2 2-6-2T at closure. The line closed to passengers on 7 September 1964 and freight on 22 May 1967. Wolverton was, and is, a railway town and the branch was much-used by workers from the famous carriage works. The branch trackbed is now a footpath, known locally as "Railway Walk". The platform edges at Bradwell and Great Linford are still visible, and the girder bridge over the Grand Union Canal at Great Linford still survives. The station site at Newport Pagnell is now covered by a housing estate, "Station Road" commemorating the former LNWR station. The railway was originally intended to be extended to Olney, on the Bedford to Northampton branch, but the scheme was abandoned in 1875, although the earthworks can still be seen for part of the way.

WOLVERTON & STONY STRATFORD

There was a roadside steam tramway between Wolverton, Stony Stratford, and Deanshanger, running for the most part on what is now the A422. The service started on 27 May 1887 and conveyed mainly workers to the LNWR Wolverton works. The Stony Stratford to Deanshanger section completely closed as early as 1889, the whole line being stopped between 1889 and 1891. The steam tramway was laid to a gauge of 3'6" and was purchased by the LNWR in 1919 as the operating company were insolvent. The 2½-mile line passed into LMS ownership at the grouping but finally closed on 4 May 1926. Steam trams could not compete with motorbuses and the general strike of 1926 finished the line off — what a wonderful set-up it would be today, if it had survived! When the tramway was opened in 1887 it was operated by two tram engines built by Krauss of Munich, being typical continental steam trams. Two more tram engines were built by Thomas Green of Leeds in 1887, and the LNWR introduced a Bagnall 0-4-0T in February 1920. The massive 100-seat, double bogie, double-deck tramcars were, at the time they ran, the largest tramcars in the British Empire. Little trace of this interesting tramway can be seen today.

CHEDDINGTON TO AYLESBURY HIGH STREET

The Cheddington to Aylesbury line was one of the earliest branch railways, the London & Birmingham main line having been opened on 9 April 1838 through Cheddington. The Aylesbury branch was officially opened on 15 June 1839 amid much celebration in the town; all shops were closed, a public holiday declared and free rides arranged to Cheddington.

After a more direct line to London had been opened by the Metropolitan in 1892 and the Great Central in 1899, the branch became of less importance to the town. BR named the station Aylesbury High St in 1950 and closed it to passengers on 2 February 1953. The line was worked at closure by an ex-LNWR 2-4-2T No 46601 working a push and pull unit. Goods traffic lasted longer on this 7-mile branch and ceased on 12 December 1963.

Today, little can be seen of the terminus at Aylesbury, the site now being a car park. The only intermediate station at Marston Gate is a private house, the platforms having been demolished.

LEIGHTON BUZZARD TO DUNSTABLE

The London & Birmingham Railway main line passed through Leighton Buzzard in 1838 and was one of Britain's first trunk lines. A branch to Dunstable, a distance of 6¾ miles, was opened on 1 June 1848. This was the principal route to the town until the arrival of the Great Northern in 1860 from Luton and Welwyn. The branch from Leighton Buzzard, having become part of the LNWR, terminated at Dunstable North, where an end-on junction was made with the GNR who also had their own station at Dunstable Town.

The passenger service was always skimpy and at the time of withdrawal on 2 July 1962 comprised only three trains per day. The trains were formed of standard two-coach push and pull units, worked by Ivatt class 2, 2-6-2 Ts. The freight service ceased on 3 April 1967.

Today, Dunstable North is built upon but the intermediate station site at Stanbridgeford, 4¼ miles from Leighton Buzzard, can still be seen (remains of the platform edges) and the old station house has been well restored. The passenger service from Hatfield to Dunstable North was discontinued on 26 April 1965 and freight on 9 October 1967.

HARPENDEN TO HEMEL HEMPSTEAD
The 8-mile long branch from Harpenden to Hemel Hempstead was opened on 16 July 1877 and worked by the Midland Railway, the service being from Luton direct via the original north curve until July 1888, when the trains were diverted to Harpenden via a new south curve. The MR introduced a railmotor service on 9 August 1905 and opened three new halts at Godwin's, Beaumont's, and Heath Park, ¾-mile beyond Hemel Hempstead. The branch was at one time physically connected to the main line at the present Hemel Hempstead (LNWR) station, but only through sidings. A through service was mooted but the MR is thought to have opposed this as the LNWR was felt to have had the better outlet both north and south. The LMS closed the branch to passengers on 16 June 1947, having arranged substitute bus services. Freight lasted until 1 July 1963 to Hemel Hempstead Midland Road, and until 1981, the line being worked by Hemelite Ltd in its last years, from Harpenden to Claydale Siding. Not much remains to be seen in Hemel Hempstead today, although the viaduct at Heath Park still remains.

Hemel Hempstead Midland Road to Boxmoor Gasworks closed to freight on 31 August 1959, including the site of Heath Park Halt and Cotterells Depot. Hertfordshire County Council have proposed to turn the trackbed of the branch into a footpath. Part of the branch is built upon by the Redbourn by-pass.

WATFORD TO ST. ALBANS
This line still thrives, having a frequent diesel multiple unit service of 22 trains each way per day. The 6½-mile long line with four intermediate stations has been severely rationalised in recent years. St Albans Abbey has no buildings apart from a waiting hut, and even no sidings. The terminus at St Albans was a very substantial building in LMS days, with an overall roof, and, apart from all the station facilities, was the terminus for another line, of GNR origin, from Hatfield. The GNR Hatfield to St Albans branch closed on 1 October 1951. The branch from Watford opened on 5 May 1858, St Albans LNWR station being named St Albans Abbey after grouping. The branch is to be electrified by May 1989.

RICKMANSWORTH CHURCH STREET AND CROXLEY GREEN
Rickmansworth Church St opened on 1 October 1862 and thrived as a commuter line until the coming of the Metropolitan Railway with a direct route to Baker St. The Rickmansworth branch was electrified in 1927 but closed on 3 March 1952. Freight traffic lasted longer, ceasing on 2 January 1967. The Croxley Green branch opened on 15 June 1912, was electrified on 30 October 1922 by the LNWR and had through trains to Broad Street until 6 June 1966, when the direct curve to Bushey closed. The service now shuttles to Watford Jcn and back. There are 15 trains per day and these run at peak hours only. Croxley Mill to Watford High St, the remaining part of the former Church St line, closed to freight in December 1980 and the track has recently been lifted (1986-7).

HARROW & WEALDSTONE TO STANMORE
This short 2-mile branch was opened as late as December 1890 and was an independent company financed locally until absorbed into the LNWR in 1899. The line was worked by the LNWR from the opening and Harrow & Wealdstone station had a bay platform at the London end to serve the branch. The one intermediate station at Belmont was opened by the LMS in 1932. The line was worked in later years by Fowler 0-4-4 tanks and Ivatt 2-6-2 tanks. The push and pull service amounted to 40 trains per day. The passenger service was cut back to Belmont on 15 September 1952 and ceased altogether from 5 October 1964. By closure the line was worked by diesel railcars including the A.C. Cars 3-car sets of 4-wheeled vehicles. Freight traffic ceased with the passenger service on 5 October 1964. Stanmore's station building was unusual as the exterior resembled a church — there was even a steeple.

HAMMERSMITH & CHISWICK (NSWJR)
The short branch to Hammersmith & Chiswick was 1½ miles long and opened on 1 May 1857. The LNWR introduced a railmotor service on 8 April 1909, and opened three intermediate halts. The railmotor service lasted until 1 January 1917 when the line was closed to passengers as part of the war economy drive to save manpower, which involved many inner suburban stations. BR closed the line completely on 3 May 1965, the final traffic on the line was fuel oil for Eastmans. The branch left the NSWJR at South Acton and ran on its own tracks from there to the terminus which was near to Stamford Brook LT (LSWR) station.

ROMFORD TO UPMINSTER & GRAYS
This suburban line was, on opening, a rural branch and has recently been electrified. The line, which was electrified on 12 May 1986, starts from a bay platform at Romford and runs three miles to Upminster. There is an intermediate station at Emerson Park which, at the time of writing, is the original LTSR edifice. The line continues on to Grays, another 6¾ miles, with an intermediate station at Ockendon. The branch still retains something of its rural character and was opened in 1892 as a blocking line to stop the Great Eastern reaching Tilbury.

THAMESHAVEN
Thameshaven Jcn to Thameshaven is a former LTSR line which now conveys oil and petrochemicals from Shell and Mobil installations. Coryton Mobil terminal did connect with the one-time Corringham Light Railway which closed on 3 March 1952. Parts of the Corringham Light Railway are still in use, worked by industrial locos.

Bedford St Johns sees a Cambridge train departing on 28 December 1966 with a lightweight multiple unit diesel hauling a vacuum fitted van which the shunter has just coupled up. Bedford St Johns was the original terminus of the Bedford Railway which was planned in the 1840s as a branch from Bletchley on the London & Birmingham main line. The Bedford Railway eventually became part of the LNWR and opened on 17 November 1846. The passenger service through to Cambridge ceased from 1 January 1968 and most of the track was lifted shortly afterwards. Bedford St Johns station was closed on 14 May 1984 and the Bletchley trains diverted to Bedford Midland station. A new Bedford St Johns has been built by Ampthill Rd bridge and is an unstaffed halt. Photograph by R. Joanes.

A relic of the former London & North Western Railway seen at Lidlington in 1986 was the signalling which was worked with Annetts Keys. The keys were inserted into the ground frame and when the signals protecting the level crossing were in the "off" position, the gates would be locked. The illustration at the top shows the open ground frame and signalman's hut. The illustration at the bottom left shows the gates being unlocked with the key, having been withdrawn from the ground frame. The illustration, below right, shows the frame with keys and Webb "clutch" levers.

Scenes on the "Oxbridge" line, (above) the topiary at Swanbourne created by the late Fred Walter outlines an LNWR 0-8-0 "super D" at the station approach. In the picture below by R. Joanes, a "Derby Lightweight" DMMU pauses at Fenny Stratford in December 1966.

Rushden station on the former Higham Ferrers branch still survives and has been restored to its former glory complete with platform furniture. The restoration has been carried out with a grant from the Local Authority and the building is now occupied by local enthusiasts who have an excellent museum, bar and restaurant. The upper photograph shows 84006 and push & pull train in BR days whilst the lower picture shows the present-day scene.

A traditional LMR branch line scene of the sixties with class 2 2-6-2T No 41222 at Great Linford looking towards Wolverton on 29 February 1964. A footpath now runs through the site of the station — photograph by R. Joanes.

Newport Pagnell station was the terminus of a branch line which was originally intended to extend towards Olney and was built as a through station. The line closed to all traffic on 22 May 1967 having closed to passengers on 7 September 1964. Photograph by Lens of Sutton.

Dunstable North with class 2, 2-6-2 T No 84002 and the Leighton Buzzard train on 20 June 1962 in the upper picture, and Stanbridgeford in the lower. The only intermediate station on this former London & Birmingham branch, Stanbridgeford was little used. Note the original low platform provided with steps. Photos by R. Joanes.

Scenes on the Buckingham to Banbury branch on 19 March 1960 with lightweight multiple unit railcars introduced by BR in 1956. The photograph above shows the train at Buckingham and the scene below shows Banbury Merton St. Merton St station has now been demolished, having ceased to handle passengers on 2 January 1961 and freight on the line to Buckingham in December 1964. Photographs by R. Joanes.

A Hertfordshire railtour by the Railway Correspondence & Travel Society in April 1958 visited the Stanmore branch (closed on 15 September 1952 — upper) and the St Albans branch (lower). The locomotive 0-4-4T No 41901 is seen crossing at Bricket Wood. This line is to be electrified in the near future.

The LMS 4F No 44441, an 0-6-0, pauses at Hemel Hempstead and is admired by 15 year old Derrick Joanes in the upper picture whilst, in the lower, 47307 shunts at Rickmansworth Church St. Both photographs taken by Roger Joanes on 3 June 1960. The Hemel Hempstead branch was unusual in that it did not terminate at a station but at a halt. Heath Park was ¾ mile beyond Hemel Hempstead, the total distance to Harpenden being 8¾ miles.

The upper photograph by John Meredith shows the exterior of Aylesbury High St on 31 January 1953. In the lower photograph by Trevor Rowe, Webb 0-6-2T No 58887 can be seen on an RCTS special on 10 October 1954. The Webb "Coal Tanks" of the LNWR dated from 1881 and the class consisted originally of 300 engines. One member of the class survives and occasionally works specials.

Stoke Bruerne (upper) on 4 May 1963 showing the line in use for wagon storage, the view is towards Towcester. This obscure part of the SMJ system ceased to have a passenger service after 1892. Stoke Bruerne station exists today as a private house, the twin station of Alcey Forest having disappeared. Photograph by J.R. Langford.

Towcester, once the centre of the SMJ system, shown here in BR days. Photo by M.A. Jose.

Stratford-on-Avon (Old Town) had become rather tatty by the time BR had withdrawn the passenger service in 1952.
A 4F 0-6-0 trundles through the station on an unfitted freight.
Photograph by M.A. Jose.

Stratford-on-Avon in the heyday of the Stratford-on-Avon & Midland Junction Railway in the early part of the century. This photograph by S.W.A. Newton of Great Central fame shows a spotless 0-6-0 No 15.

Blakesley station on the SMJR "main line" was the junction for the 15 inch gauge Blakesley Hall Light Railway which was $\frac{3}{4}$ mile long and conveyed coal to Blakesley Hall. The line was lifted in 1940.
Photo by Mowat.

Salford Priors in the upper photograph, a classic view of a Midland country station with Midland lamp, seat, and ground frame. Photograph by J.R. Langford. In the lower photograph a view of Broom Junction from the train window, photograph by M.A. Jose.

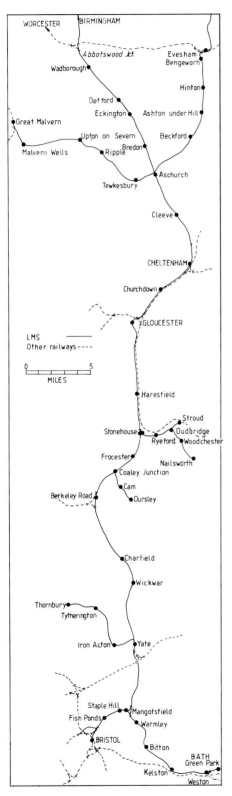

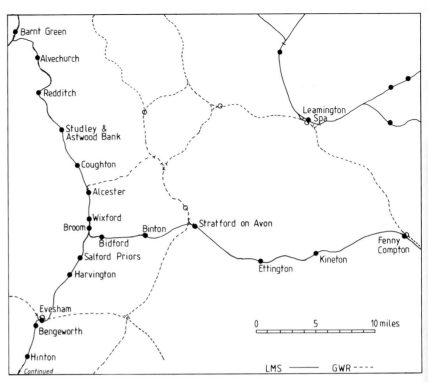

The cramped and difficult to operate station at Dursley which was tucked away around the back of the town and difficult to find. The station was squeezed in between factories and had one or two Midland accessories such as the Midland lamp standard and station seat. The line closed to passengers on 10 September 1962 under Western Region auspices. Freight traffic lasted until 13 July 1970. The station has now been completely demolished as well as the intermediate station at Cam. Photograph by Lens of Sutton.

The changing fortunes of Ripple station, an intermediate on the Upton-on-Severn branch of the former Midland Railway which closed to passengers on 14 August 1961 and freight on 1 July 1963. In the above view taken by Hugh Ballantyne on 16 May 1957, 3F No 43754 hauls a single coach on the 5.45 pm Upton-on-Severn to Ashchurch. The line had been singled by the time the upper photograph had been taken. In the lower picture (taken recently) the station has been turned into a private house with an extensive flower garden laid out by Mrs Fullerlove, who got the idea from Petworth on the Midhurst branch of the LBSCR. Another item of interest is the station fence with the contractor's starting and finishing date in 1892. The wooden fence is of non-standard Midland design, having been constructed by the contractors.

*Nailsworth in Midland days with a spick and span platform and plenty of railway staff in the upper picture and Stroud (Wallbridge) in th
lower. The station at Nailsworth still exists as a private house but the building at Stroud has now been demolished. Both lines closed to
passengers on 8 June 1949 and freight on 1 June 1966. Nailsworth photo by Lens of Sutton.*

A typical Midland scene on BR during the mid fifties shows Burton allocated 4F (built 1928) No 44526 plodding along the main line at Coaley Jcn. The train is of general goods with cattle vans leading. Behind the tall Midland signal and ballast train can be seen the Dursley branch platform with a Midland starting signal.

Tytherington, with the daily goods to Thornbury on 15 March 1962, headed by a 4F 0-6-0. Although the buildings have been demolished, the platform still exists and so does the approach footpath from the street. The line closed to passengers on 19 June 1944.

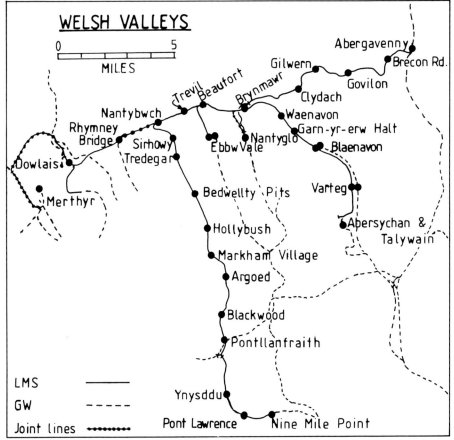

Nine Mile Point on the occasion of an SLS railtour in South Wales stopped for water with 0-6-0 pannier tank No 6434 in unlined BR black and a push & pull unit of GWR origin. The station nameboard is of interest as it is an LMS "Hawkseye" in black and yellow — the LMS colours. Nine Mile Point was where the LMS Sirhowy Valley line met the GWR from Newport. The name originated from the fact that the junction between the LNWR and GWR was nine miles from Newport. The Sirhowy Tramroad opened in 1805 and joined with the Monmouthshire Canal company's tramroad (later GWR) at Nine Mile Point. The Sirhowy Tramroad was horse-worked at the outset and had a passenger service which became steam hauled. Photograph taken 12 July 1958.

ABERGAVENNY TO MERTHYR

The 24½ mile long railway from Abergavenny to Merthyr High Street was a protégé of the LNWR and an unusual piece of railway engineering at that. The railway ran up and down mountains with gradients as steep as 1 in 34 and connected all the valley railways at the northern end. The railway was opened from Abergavenny to Brynmawr on 29 September 1862. Brynmawr to Nantybwch followed on 1 March 1864, Nantybwch to Rhymney on 5 September 1871, and Rhymney Bridge to Dowlais (Ivor Jcn) on 1 January 1873. The LNWR eventually gained access to Merthyr High Street on 9 June 1879, buying joint ownership of the existing Brecon & Merthyr line from Morlais Jcn. Nantybwch to Rhymney via Rhymney Bridge was jointly owned with the Rhymney Railway. The present Brecon Mountain Railway terminates above the old Morlais tunnel adjacent to one of the ventilation chimneys, all of which can still be seen today.

The Abergavenny to Merthyr line conveyed coal traffic from the valleys to the industrial north, the high grade Welsh coal being in demand for industry and shipping. The LNWR exercised running powers over the Rhymney Railway from Rhymney Bridge to Cardiff Docks. The peak loading was reached in 1917 with coal trains running over the system day and night conveying 5,000 tons per day. The line was well known for its tortuous curves and steep gradients for which the LNWR built a special class of 0-8-4 tank engines. The line was also the last resort of the Webb "Coal Tank" 0-6-2s as well as the standard LNWR 0-8-0 tender engines. The shed at Abergavenny was reputed to house 100 engines in its heyday. Brecon Road was also the District Traffic HQ as well as the control for the area.

The last train from Abergavenny to Merthyr ran on 5 January 1958, hauled appropriately by the last "Coal Tank" No 58926 and Super D" No 49121, an LNWR 0-8-0. The "Coal Tank", built in 1887, has been preserved and still runs on the occasional special — the last special of note being the "Cam 80" private charter from Shrewsbury in 1986. The last train from Abergavenny to Merthyr could be described as a "Cam 50", or "Cam 52" to be more precise.

The author and his cronies witnessed the departure of the last regular passenger train from Merthyr High Street on Saturday, 4 January 1958. After the train had departed, a taxi was hired which hared through the dank streets of Merthyr to Dowlais High Street. Having beaten the train by several minutes, the LNWR tickets on sale were purchased well in time to board the train to Abergavenny. The same tickets were sold on the special last train on Sunday, 5 January — the tickets being LNWR first-class blank priv.

The line closed to all traffic from 6 January 1958 with the exception of the Nantybwch to Beafort section which remained open to freight until 5 November 1959. Brynmawr to Nantyglo closed to passengers on 30 April 1962, and freight on 4 December 1963.

Today, a large part of the former railway is now the A465 "Heads of The Valleys Road" built over the trackbed from Beafort to Dowlais Top. Nantybwch viaduct still exists as well as the LNWR culverts under the road. In addition to the road, there is a footpath from Llanfoist to Gilwern. Platforms and station houses survive at Govilon, Gilwern, Clydach, and the platforms at Gelli Felen Halt. Brecon Road is an Electricity Board car park and Brynmawr goods shed survives on an industrial estate.

BRYNMAWR TO BLAENAVON

The LNWR built a branch from Brynmawr to Blaenavon which extended to Abersychan & Talywain and made connection with the GWR. The railway opened for freight on 1 November 1869 and to passengers on 1 January 1870 to Blaenavon (later High Level), the extension to Abersychan being opened in 1877. The distance from Talywain Jcn was 8½ miles from Brynmawr, the last ½-mile being jointly owned with the GWR. Brynmawr to Talywain closed to passengers on 5 May 1941, the passenger trains latterly being worked by the GWR through from Brynmawr to Pontypool or Newport. The GWR had their own branch from Newport to Blaenavon which duplicated the LNWR north of Pontypool Crane Street. Blaenavon to Brynmawr closed to all traffic on 24 June 1954. The line was used for wagon storage for several years afterwards. A 2-mile section from Furnace Siding to Blaenavon was even reopened between 1972 and 1975 by Derek Couch Ltd. It was to Blaenavon shed that the late J.M. Dunn was banished during the 1926 strike, coming from Willesden Jcn.

THE PONTYPOOL & BLAENAVON RAILWAY

This is a new preserved steam railway and operates from Furnace Siding to Whistle Inn with the intention of extending southwards to Varteg Road on the former Blaenavon LNWR branch. The P&BR claim to be the highest preserved railway in Britain at 1,300 feet.

The railway has a Peckett 0-6-0ST, a Barclay 0-4-0ST, and an 0-6-0ST "Austerity" built by R.S.H. and rebuilt by Hunslets. More interesting amongst the industrials is an 0-6-0 pannier tank "Brookfield" built by Bagnall in 1940 with outside cylinders to metre gauge. This locomotive was intended for a Turkish metre gauge railway but was re-gauged to standard for use in Britain. The railway also possesses a Fowler DM 0-6-0 used for shunting. The Barry haulks arrived in August 1987, being five ex-GWR locos purchased for the railway by a Hertfordshire businessman. There is also the Big Pit Museum, a preserved coal mine which visitors can descend into if they wish.

The railway has been open for four years but has a long way to go yet, though the future does look promising.

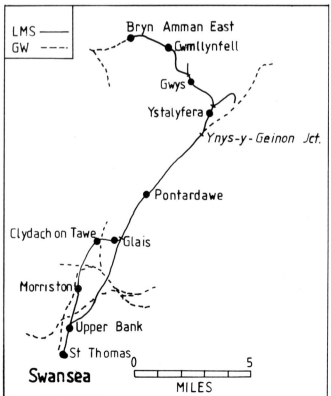

The Midland in South Wales, Brynamman East *(above) in 1958 and Ynys-y-Geinon Jcn (below) with Midland bracket signal and signal box.*

Map labels:

LMS ——
GW – – –

Bryn Amman East
Cwmllynfell
Gwys
Ystalyfera
Ynys-y-Geinon Jct.
Pontardawe
Clydach on Tawe
Glais
Morriston
Upper Bank
St Thomas
Swansea

0   5
MILES

EBBW VALE TO EBBW VALE JUNCTION

The distance from Brynmawr to Ebbw Vale was 3½ miles over which the LNWR worked a railmotor service with 0-6-2 "Coal Tanks", the service in 1922 being 15 return trips per day. The distance as the crow flies betwween the two towns is about 1½ miles. The line was opened by the LNWR on 1 September 1867, BR closed it to passengers on 2 April 1951 — the final service having dwindled to four trains per day. The line was traversed by the SLS special last train on 5 January 1958. Freight services were withdrawn on 2 November 1959, the trains having been worked via Nantybwch which closed to Beaufort on the same day. Ebbw Vale High Level, as it was known by BR, has been partly built over and absorbed into the new A4046 road which has — for one direction only — absorbed ¼-mile of the trackbed.

NANTYBWCH TO NINE MILE POINT (SIRHOWY VALLEY)

The Sirhowy Valley branch was acquired by the LNWR and was 15½ miles long from Nantybwch to a location called Nine Mile Point — known as such through being nine miles from Newport. The LNWR connected with the GWR there and ran through trains from Nantybwch to Newport. The railway had an early start in life, opening in 1805 as a tramway known as the "Sirhowy Tramroad" which ran from Tredegar to Newport. The junction at Nine Mile Point was where the Sirhowy Tramroad joined with the Monmouthshire Canal Co's tramroad. The line was horse-worked from opening until 1829, the passenger service commencing in 1822. The LNWR eventually acquired the line in 1876, having built a connection at Nantybwch in 1868. The Sirhowy Railway Co modernised the old tramway and brought it up to main line standard in June 1865.

The line was one of the most prosperous valley lines during the heyday of steam coal. Many private colleries connected with the branch and the coal traffic was heavy. The LNWR 0-8-4 tanks were used as well as the GI 0-8-0s and 0-6-2 side tanks. There was a sizeable loco shed at Tredegar with four roads and, at grouping, there were 24 locomotives allocated. In BR days the passenger service was withdrawn on 13 June 1960. Freight traffic was withdrawn from Nantybwch to Sirhowy on 13 June 1960 and Sirhowy to Tredegar on 4 November 1963. Freight traffic lasted south to Pontllanfraith until 30 April 1969, and Pontllanfraith (Tredegar Jcn Lower) to Risca until 4 May 1970. A feature of the line during passenger days was the running of specials to seaside resorts during the summer. The author travelled on an unusual excursion on 13 July 1958 from Tredegar to Barry Island. The train was hauled by an LNWR 0-8-0 and travelled via Bird in Hand Jcn, Penrhos Jcns, Walnut Tree Viaduct, Wenvoe, and Cadoxton. The train left Tredegar at 09.47 and arrived at Barry Island at 12.00 noon. A footpath now runs from Nine Mile Point to Cross Keys, and the top part of the line is now a road.

BRYNAMMAN EAST TO SWANSEA (ST. THOMAS)

The Midland Railway reached South Wales via extensive running powers over the GWR, it's own line from Hereford to Three Cocks Jcn and the Cambrian, Brecon & Merthyr, and Neath & Brecon Railways. Colbren Jcn, on the Neath & Brecon main line to Ynis-y-Geiron Jcn was opened on 10 November 1873 by the Neath & Brecon Railway. Swansea St Thomas to Pontardawe had opened in 1852 as the Swansea Vale Railway, a private line opened without an Act of Parliament. The line was extended north of Pontardawe on 1 January 1864 to Brynamman with a connection to the GWR branch. The Midland worked the SVR from 1874 and acquired it in 1876. The passenger service from Swanseas St Thomas to Brynamman East was withdrawn by BR on 25 September 1950. The 1922 Bradshaw shows six trains per day on the branch and three through from Brecon worked by Midland trains from Hereford. The Midland at one time operated a through service from Birmingham to Swansea via this route but the LMS withdrew the Hereford to Swansea service in 1931. Colbren Jcn to Pontardawe, which had become worked by the GWR, closed to passengers from 12 September 1932. The loop line via Morriston was opened on 1 March 1875, passenger trains being routed this way from the original direct SVR which then became goods only. When the Brynamman to Swansea passenger service was withdrawn in 1950, Clydach to Glais was demolished and Glais viaduct dismantled (1955).

The Brynamman East branch closed to all traffic back to Gurnos on 28 September 1964 and from Ynyscedwyn Colliery to Llansamlet on 30 April 1968. The Morriston loop line closed completely from Glais to Clydach on 25 September 1950 and later closed back to Morriston East on 12 July 1965. The Ynys-y-Geinon Jcn to Colbren Jcn section of the former Neath & Brecon closed completely on 20 February 1967. The last piece of Miland line from Swansea Eastern Depot to Morriston East (BSC) was disused from 24 May 1983.

Today, Ystalyfera to Gwys is now the A4067/68 road, Morriston East is part of the A4067 and Pontardawe to Ynys-y-Geinon an informal footpath.

THE SWANSEA VALE RAILWAY

The 1½-mile section of the former Midland Railway line between Six Pit and Upper Bank has been taken over by the newly created Swansea Vale Railway, a new preservation project. The project enjoys the support of the Swansea City Council and limited grants. The SVR intend to create a Midland station at Upper Bank and a GWR one at Six Pit. The railway has acquired an ex-GWR 2-8-0T No 4270 from Barry and also possesses an 0-6-0ST No 3829, a Hunslet "Austerity". On bank holidays in 1987, the society borrowed a Barclay 0-4-0ST "Victory" ex-Stewarts & Lloyds from the Caerphilly Railway Society.

Nantgaredig station in this August 1962 scene has changed little over the years. The station nameboard is still in the LMS black on yellow but is of LNWR origin. The signal is of LNWR origin on a concrete post but the Western Region have provided an 0-6-0 pannier tank to work the trains. The station nameboard still exists today and the station building is now a private house, having been extended to two floors. The line was closed to all traffic on 9 September 1963. Today there are relics to be seen at the site of each station, including an LNWR lower quadrant signal. The 14¼ mile Llandilo to Carmarthen line was opened in 1865 as part of the Llanelly Railway, a railway which became divided between the LNWR and GWR, the Llandilo to Carmarthen being acquired by the LNWR. An unusual relic at Nantgaredig, apart from the station building, is a grounded LMS bogie van body No M 37717 M.

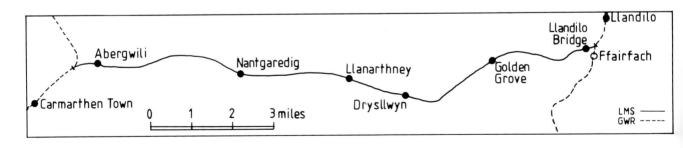

GOWERTON TO LLANMORLAIS

This branch, 4¾ miles in length, was constructed partly over the abandoned Penclawdd Canal which closed in 1814. The line was opened for passengers and freight in January 1868 and was acquired by the LNWR in September 1873. The line was extended from Penclawdd to Llanmorlais, a distance of two miles, on 1 March 1884. The pre-grouping train service consisted of six trains per day with an extra on Saturdays. The train service included a through train operation to Swansea but fell victim to competing bus services and was withdrawn by the LMS on 5 January 1931. Freight trains ran under BR until 2 September 1957. A part of the line from Crofty to Llanmorlais is an informal footpath; the station house at Llanmorlais is still in existence, and Penclawdd has now been restored as a house.

LLANDILO TO CARMARTHEN

The LNWR served Swansea via the Central Wales line, 115¼ miles from Shrewsbury, with three trains from Liverpool, Manchester, and even Euston. A branch was constructed from Llandilo to Carmarthen, a distance of 14¼ miles, and opened in 1865. Opened as a section of the Llanelly Railway which was divided between the LNWR and GWR in 1867–73, the branch became incorporated into the Swansea & Carmarthen Railway. The S&CR became worked by the LNWR in 1871, being purchased in 1891. On formation of the LMS in 1923 there were six trains per day each way, and at closure in 1963 there were only four. One train ran through on Saturdays from Carmarthen to Shrewsbury. The line was closed to all traffic from 9 September 1963 by which time the trains had become "Great Westernised", using pannier tanks and ex-GWR stock. There were at closure several relics of the LNWR including signals and LNWR ground frames with Webb levers. Several relics survive today and the LNWR nameboard can still be seen at Nantgaredig which has been rebuilt into a private house. A grounded LMS bogie van body No M37717M can also be seen at Nantgaredig. Golden Grove was one of the few BR stations that doubled as a post office. Abergwilli has been sold and awaits renovation, Llanarthney survives as a house with name, Dryslwyn also has an LNWR box, and Golden Grove has a lower quadrant signal and inhabited station house. Whitenill platform remains in situ.

THREE COCKS JUNCTION TO HEREFORD

The first railway from Brecon to Eardisley was opened as a horse-worked railway in 1816 known as the Hay Railway, the line of which ran through to Burlingjobb near Dolyhir, New Radnor. The railway was 3'6" gauge and connected with the canal at Brynich Bridge, Brecon, and the Kington Railway at Eardisley. Present-day remains include a tramroad bridge at Hay-on Wye still in situ. The railway from Hereford to Eardisley opened for passengers on 30 June 1863 as the Hereford, Hay, & Brecon Railway. From 19 September 1864, through services ran from Hay to Brecon over the rebuilt Hay Railway using the Mid Wales, and Brecon & Merthyr lines. A curiosity was the amalgamation of the HH&BR with the Brecon & Merthyr Railway in 1865 and disamalgamation in 1868. The amalgamation had not been approved by the preference shareholders of the B&MR and the Midland Railway stepped in to lease the line. The Midland took over the line from 1 October 1869 as an extension of its newly acquired running powers over the GWR from Worcester to Hereford. As a consequence, the isolated Hereford to Three Cocks Jcn section became part of the LMS system. The Midland ran through trains to Swansea via this route but the LMS discontinued the Hereford to Swansea service from 1 January 1931.

The limited service of four passenger trains per day over the 26¼ miles from Hereford to Three Cocks Jcn was withdrawn by BR on 31 December 1962, the same day as the nearby Mid Wales line. Freight traffic ceased on the same day from Three Cocks Jcn to Eardisley but lingered on until 28 September 1964 from Eardisley to Hereford. The line was unusual in that it possessed a private station at Westmoor, situated between Credenhill and Moorhampton 6¾ miles from Hereford. The station was built for a local landowner and was in use until BR times. The building still exists with an odd Italianate tower.

Other remains to be seen include a low timber viaduct between Hay-on Wye and Whitney-on-Wye, a brick goods shed at Hay-on-Wye, platforms at Whitney and one platform building at Kinnersley. The wooden station building, goods shed, and GWR six-wheeled carriage body can be found at Eardisley, whilst the buildings have vanished at Credenhill. A short length of platform remains at Moorhampton, and Hereford Moorfields is occupied by Balmers Sidings. Several Midland mileposts can be discerned on the route.

THE BANGOR TO AFONWEN BRANCH

The line started as the Bangor & Carnarvon Railway and the Carnarvonshire Railway, the former from Menai Bridge and the latter from Carnarvon to Afon Wen. Both railways were independent and had separate terminals at Carnarvon. The first section to be opened was from Bangor to Port Dinorwic on 10 March 1852. There was a short branch of one mile from the line to Port Dinorwic Quay to serve the Padarn Railway, the branch to the quay being opened to goods only in 1857. The Carnarvonshire Railway on to Afon Wen was opened on 2 September 1867 but the railways were not joined up with a single station until 1870. The section to Penygroes was largely built over the former 3'6" gauge Nantlle Railway of 1828 which was horse-worked and conveyed slate to Carnarvon Quay. The LNWR acquired the Bangor & Carnarvon and the Carnarvonshire by 1870, but the Cambrian had built their main line to Pwllheli preventing the LNWR going beyond Afon Wen.

Afon Wen was a remote railway junction serving a very small community half a mile distant, but a change-over point for all passengers journeying northwards from Portmadoc. The LNWR line was double track from Menai Bridge on the Chester to Holyhead main line to Caernarvon, renamed thus by the LMS in 1925 from the LNWR's Carnarvon. Caernarvon to Afon Wen was single track throughout and closed to all traffic on 7 December 1964. Tracklifting north from Afon Wen halted at Llanwnda for some months in 1969. The four miles of track from Caernarvon to Llanwnda was used to stable empty stock for the special trains to the 1969 investiture of the Prince of Wales. Passenger trains lasted from Caernarvon to Menai Bridge until 5 January 1970 and freightliners until 5 February 1972, the line being used by freightliners from 1970 to 1972 as a result of the fire damage to the Bridge in May 1970.

At Afon Wen the station house is the only surviving building out of this former three-platform station and junction in the middle of nowhere. The LMS used their side of the station — the north face of the up island platform — and GWR trains used the rest. Chivilog was a single platform station with an LNWR open frame but this station site is now built upon. Llangybi still has the original stone building whilst Ynys still has a house formerly used by the stationmaster. Brynkir and Pant Glas have been demolished, but a cycle path now runs from Brynkir to Dinas and this is being extended to Caernarvon. The cycle path is tarred and runs along the railway trackbed — it looks like a road from a distance. Penygroes, Groeslon, Llanwnda and Caernarvon stations have all been demolished, the latter site now a car park.

A little known survival is Dinas Jcn where the Welsh Highland Railway met the LMS. Many of the buildings survive and the site is worth a visit. The station buildings, goods shed, station house, and narrow gauge bridge under the road may all be seen. The buildings are used as a council depot. The Welsh Highland, closed in 1936 to passengers and 1937 to freight, was 2'0" gauge and ran through to Portmadoc. Dinas Jcn closed as an intermediate station on 10 September 1951. Port Dinorwic station buildings still exist and are used by a stationery wholesaler. Port Dinorwic Harbour has been landscaped and turned into a yacht marina, being unrecognisable from the slate terminus of former years. Griffiths Crossing station, closed in 1937, has been demolished but the remote and picturesque Treborth, closed in 1959, has been converted into a private house — "Station House".

PENYGROES TO NANTLLE

The Nantlle branch opened as a horse-drawn tramway conveying slate to Caernarvon and was opened in 1828 using a gauge of 3'6". The railway also operated a passenger service. The LNWR purchased the railway and converted most of it to standard gauge. The Nantlle branch of 1½ miles was opened to standard gauge and steam-worked from 1872, the LNWR working the line as a branch from Penygroes. The LNWR-built Nantlle branch, was almost wholly on a new alignment from Penygroes station to Nantlle station. (Nantlle station was in the village of Talysarn, Nantlle village being two miles further up the valley.) The LNWR introduced a railmotor to the line but passenger trains were withdrawn during the First World War. The LMS finally withdrew passenger services on 8 August 1932. Freight lasted under BR until 2 December 1963. A curiosity was that the original narrow-gauge, horse-drawn tramway also lasted until 1963 above Nantlle station, as the quarries were connected to the BR station by the original tramway until closure. The line was last traversed by a railtour organised by the SLS/MLS on 20 October 1963, which included the horse-worked tramway. The station building at Nantlle is now a community centre, and the branch trackbed is mainly now occupied by the B4418 road.

CAERNARVON TO LLANBERIS

The Llanberis branch, opened by the LNWR on 1 July 1869, had a separate but parallel track from the Afon Wen line into Caenarvon which was nine miles long. Passenger trains ceased on 12 September 1932 and freight on 7 September 1964. The LMSR used observation coaches on the trains, one of which is in use on the Bluebell Railway and is restored to the original LNWR "plum and spilt milk" livery. Excursions were run by BR in the summer from Rhyl in post war years, the train being named "The Snowdonian". The excursions in the summer ran from 1932 to 1939 and 1946 to 1963, the last BR excursion being on 7 September 1963. The SLS/MLS railtour which visited Nantlle on 20 October 1963 also traversed the Llanberis branch and was possibly the last passenger train of all. Llanberis station today is an arts and crafts centre. The short-lived Padarn Halt near Llanberis has disappeared, while the by-pass road has been built over the site of Cwm-y-Glo station. Pontrhythallt station is now a private house and Pontrug, which closed in 1930, has become engulfed in trees and bushes except for the station house and approach road which still exists.

GAERWEN TO AMLWCH

The Amlwch branch still prospers although with freight trains only — the passenger service having been discontinued on 7 December 1964. The branch opened to passengers on 3 June 1867 throughout, having started out as the Anglesey Central Railway and been bought for a song by the LNWR.

The trains that run today are from the Amlwch Associated Octel Works terminal, to Stanlow Refineries, conveying a lead-based petrol additive for use in petroleum refining.

The station buildings at Amlwch have been demolished and a road has been built over the site. The stations at Rhosgoch and Llanerchymedd have been demolished but the buildings at Llangwyllog and Llangefni are private houses. Holland Arms station building survives as well as the station house.

HOLLAND ARMS TO RED WHARF BAY

Red Wharf Bay & Benllech, opened on 24 May 1909 and served by LNWR "motor trains", was built as a light railway. The railway was conceived in the pre-motor age, which was unfortunate as the terminal was some distance from both Benllech and Red Wharf Bay. The terminus had an LNWR wooden single platform with waiting room and booking office combined. There were small, timber intermediate halts at Llanbedrgoch, Pentraeth, Rhydysaint and Ceint, all having now vanished. The passenger service ceased on 22 September 1930 and freight on 3 April 1950.

BANGOR TO BETHESDA

The Bethesda Jcn to Bethesda branch was opened by the LNWR on 1 July 1884, and was 4¼ miles long. Passenger services over the single track line were withdrawn on 3 December 1951 by BR. The line was built to tap slate traffic but the Penrhyn Quarry proprietors preferred to use their own transport via Port Penrhyn and the Penrhyn Railway. Limited slate and freight traffic was carried, in addition to passengers on this LNWR branch. (Two locomotives of the Penrhyn Railway — "Blanche" and "Linda", built by Hunslet in 1893 and now running as 2-4-0 tender tanks — can still be seen at work on the Ffestiniog Railway.) Freight services lasted on the Besthesda branch until 7 October 1963, the last train being an SLS railtour on 20 October 1963. There were two intermediate stopping points on the line — Felin Hen Halt and Tregarth. Tregarth station buildings are well preserved, being a good example of LNWR wooden standard construction of 100 years ago. The station is now the local community centre. Bethesda station site is now occupied by a social club, and parts of the trackbed are being converted into a public footpath.

PORT PENRHYN

The Chester & Holyhead Railway opened a short 1¼ mile branch from Penrhyn Sidings on the main line near Llandegai Tunnel to Penrhyn Quay. The branch, goods only, ran parallel to the 1'11½" Penrhyn Railway which brought slate down from Penrhyn Quarries for shipment from the Port. The branch was opened in 1852 and closed by the London Midland Region on 4 March 1963. Port Penrhyn to Tregarth on the former Bethesda branch is now a footpath which includes parts of the LNWR line and the Penrhyn Railway.

LLANDUDNO TO BLAENAU FFESTINIOG

The single-track line from Llandudno to Blaenau Ffestiniog is 28 miles long and runs through the Conwy Valley. BR now issue a tourist brochure for 20 pence describing "British Rail's Beautiful Conwy Valley Line". The railway now has a joint station with the Ffestiniog Railway and provides a through route from North Wales to the Cambrian Coast by connecting with the narrow gauge. The line was opened by 22 July 1878 throughout and consisted of numerous engineering works including the 2¼-mile long Ffestiniog tunnel, the longest tunnel wholly in Wales, and one of Britain's longest. The LNWR terminated at Blaenau Ffestiniog North station, about ¾-mile from the Central station on the GWR line from Bala Jcn. A new standard gauge link between the two was built about 1961, parallel to the then-derelict Ffestiniog Railway track. The GWR line closed in 1961, south of Trawsfynydd Lake Halt, but is still used to Trawsfynydd Lake. Recently a new interchange station has been built at Blaenau Ffestiniog servicing the standard and reopened narrow gauge. The new station is approximately where the old GWR station once stood.

The service has been improved recently by the introduction of "Pacer" units, well known for their squealing flanges. The line still retains something of a rural branch line atmosphere as all the stations are still in use, although unstaffed. At Roman Bridge the station buildings remain as a private residence, while at Dolwyddelan and Pont-y-Pant only waiting huts suffice for the passengers. The large station buildings survive at Betws-y-Coed which also has a private railway museum and 7¼" gauge miniature railway on the goods yard site. Llanrwst has the only signalbox on the line, a fine relic of the LNWR and worth a visit. Dolgarrog and Glan Conwy are unstaffed halts but the buildings remain at Glan Conwy. The best station to visit is the staffed Tal-y-Cafn, just about as near as you can get to the traditional country station, once so common on BR. The buildings are intact and the flowerbeds well maintained at this remote spot near the Afon Conwy. The new Ffestiniog station, known as Blaenau Ffestiniog Central, was opened by BR on 22 March 1982.

DYSERTH

The Prestatyn to Dyserth line was 3¼ miles long with three intermediate halts at Chapel St, Rhuddlan Rd, and Meliden. The railway opened for goods only on 1 September 1869, the traffic conveyed being coal to the lead and and zinc mines at Meliden and iron ore outwards. The quarries at Dyserth also produced limestone which was conveyed until 1973, the last mineral train running on 8 September 1973. The LNWR and L&YR pioneered the use of railmotors which were a combined locomotive and coach worked by driver and fireman with a conductor/guard. These units were introduced to combat bus and tramway competition in rural and suburban areas. Dyserth was the first LNWR branch to be worked by railmotors on 26 August 1905. Many other railway companies following suit during the 1905–1914 period.

The train had to reverse out of Prestatyn station bay platform in order to traverse the branch. Access to the train was from rail level at all stations including Prestatyn, a break with traditional British practice. The LNWR opened a new halt at Meliden Golf Course in 1922 known as St Melyd Golf Links Halt. The LMS replaced the LNWR railmotor with a push and pull locomotive worked train after grouping (1923), but withdrew the passenger service on 22 September 1930. There was a proposal to extend the line onto the village of Trelawnyd (Newmarket) and some of the earthworks can still be seen today. Construction had commenced in 1883 but was abandoned on the extension shortly afterwards. The track on the Prestatyn to Dyserth section has now been lifted and the trackbed is a footpath, although this may be unofficial.

HOLYWELL TOWN

Holywell Jcn to Holywell Town was 1¾ miles in length and opened on 1 July 1912 by the chairman of the LNWR, Sir Gilbert Claughton. Unusually, the line replaced an earlier LNWR motor-bus route. The main feature of the line was the severe gradient of 1 in 27, the trains being worked as rail motors or push and pull. The motive power in use on the line at closure was a Webb 0-6-2 "Coal Tank" with one coach. Closure to all traffic occurred on 6 September 1954. The terminus at Holywell was situated awkwardly under a road overbridge, access to the station being by a twisting footpath. An unusual feature at Holywell Jcn was the Chester & Holyhead Railway fare table which survived well into BR days. The Holywell Town branch was constructed over the former Holywell Railway which was a mineral railway dating from the 1870s which the LNWR purchased in 1891. There was one intermediate halt at St Winifrides, half a mile from Holywell Town.

RHYL TO CORWEN

The first section of this line from Rhyl to Denbigh was opened as a single track railway on 5 October 1858 known as the Vale of Clwyd Railway. The distance was 10 miles from Rhyl to Denbigh. A branch to Foryd Pier, 1¼ miles in length, was opened in 1865 by the Vale of Clwyd, and closed by BR on 4 April 1959. The independent Vale of Clwyd Railway was taken over by the LNWR in 1868 and connection was made at Denbigh with the railway from Mold, opened on 11 September 1869. BR withdrew passenger services from Rhyl to Denbigh on 19 September 1955.

Southwards from Denbigh the line to Corwen started as the Denbigh, Ruthin & Corwen Railway, a distance of 18¾ miles. The line was opened on 15 September 1865 throughout. The DR&CR was not taken over by the LNWR until 1 July 1879 and until that date possessed its own locomotives and rolling stock. Passenger services between Ruthin and Corwen were withdrawn on 2 February 1953, the area being very sparsely populated. BR ran a tour train entitled the "North Wales Land Cruise" over the Rhyl to Corwen line during the summer from 1951 until 8 September 1961. The train was double-headed by two class 2, 2-6-0s and consisted of an intriguing variety of coaches of LMS and LNWR vintage. Some of the coaches came from the LMS set that went to America, some from the Royal Train and some from LMS "club trains". The tour was arranged so that a running commentary was given, mentioning local landmarks and history. The passenger service from Ruthin to Denbigh ceased on 30 April 1962.

BR closed the section from Corwen to Ruthin on 30 April 1962, Ruthin to Denbigh on 1 March 1965, and Denbigh to Rhyl on 1 January 1968, to all traffic. Of the stations along the line, Gwyddelwern and Nantclwyd have been demolished, Derwen is a private house, and Eyarth a nicely restored guest house with a few pre-grouping relics and a swimming pool. Ruthin now has a craft centre on the site of the station, Rhewl is a private house and Llanrhaiadr has been demolished. Denbigh is now Townsend Engineering, and St Asaph the Vale of Clwyd Farmers Co-operative offices. Trefnant and Rhuddlan have both been demolished.

DENBIGH TO CHESTER (MOLD & DENBIGH JCN TO SALTNEY FERRY)

This railway, which was 29¼ miles from Chester, included 3¾ miles running on the main Chester to Holyhead line as far as Mold Jcn (Saltney Ferry). The first section from Mold Jcn to Mold opened on 14 August 1849 as the Mold Railway. The Mold Railway was in turn taken over by the LNWR after absorbing the Chester & Holyhead Railway in 1858. Mold was the terminus of the line until the inaugural trains ran to Denbigh on the Mold & Denbigh Jcn Railway on 12 September 1869. The Mold & Denbigh Jcn Railway had great difficulty in getting to Denbigh as the LNWR had already acquired the Vale of Clwyd from Rhyl. BR withdrew passenger trains from Denbigh to Chester on 30 April 1962, although workmen's trains ran until 2 September 1963 between Broughton and Chester. Rhydymwyn to Denbigh closed to all traffic on 30 April 1962. Freight services were withdrawn from Rhydymwyn to Mold on 1 January 1968, reinstated, and finally withdrawn, the line being lifted by the mid seventies. Mold station still stands although demolition is imminent; the station site is about to be redeveloped as a giant supermarket. Mold Jcn (on the main line) to Hope Jcn (Penyffordd) closed to freight on 2 February 1970. The freight traffic from Mold (Synthite Siding) to Penyffordd, the last section of the former Chester to Denbigh branch to be used, ceased on 3 July 1986. Rails were removed during the winter of 1986/1987.

On the line today, Bodfari station is a private house and caravan park, Caerwys is a timber yard with the statiaon buildings used as an office, and Nannerch has been obliterated by road works; Rhydymwyn is a house, but Mold awaits demolition. Llong and Hope are private houses complete with nameboards, and Saltney Ferry, along with Kinnerton, has been demolished. Broughton & Bretton station is now a private house and it was from here that Gladstone, the former British prime minister, made his last journey. An interesting feature of the line was the interchange station at Hope Exchange between the LNWR and the WM&CQR, the railways being on two different levels. There was no public access other than by a footpath, the two-level station being closed on 1 September 1958. Kinnerton station sold London & North Western Railway tickets until closure in 1962.

MOLD TO BRYMBO & COED TALON

The Ffrith branch from Hope (Ffrith Jcn) to Coed Talon, a distance of 2½ miles, was opened on 14 September 1849 and included a 1 in 33 gradient. The line, which was used by mineral trains only, closed completely after 29 July 1934 when a freight train became derailed. The track was lifted in 1935 by the LMS.

The line from Mold southwards to Coed Talon was opened by the LNWR on 3 July 1870, and on to Brymbo on 27 January 1882 for freight only, passenger services not starting until 1 January 1892 from Mold to Coed Talon. The LNWR extended passenger trains to Brymbo on 15 November 1897, where connection was made with the GWR. The July 1922 Bradshaw shows four trains daily between Mold and Brymbo, a distance of 8½ miles. The trains were one class only and possibly push and pull worked, passenger services being withdrawn by BR on 27 March 1950. Mold (Tryddyn Jcn) to Coed Talon closed to freight traffic on 22 July 1963, Coed Talon to Ffrith having closed to all traffic on 27 March 1950. The section from Coed Talon to Brymbo was jointly owned by the LNWR and GWR and known as the Wrexham & Minera Joint Railway. Joint ownership commenced 44 chains north of Llanfynydd station, according to the Railway Clearing House map.

Abergwili, on the Llandilo to Carmarthen branch of the former LNWR, with a departing train and the open ground frame being unlocked by the railman in charge on 8 August 1962. The Llandilo to Carmarthen line of 14¼ miles was closed completely on 9 September 1963. The open ground frame was a speciality of the LNWR signalling department that had evolved at Crewe during the 1870s and was in use on minor lines on the system. The LNWR had started out with contractors signalling but as the system increased in size the railway eventually built all required signalling components. The Midland and Great Western Railways also created their own signalling from complete signal boxes down to tiny ground frames. The LMS and BR perpetuated the LNWR signalling practices but in this view a mixture has taken place due to the fact that the station illustrated had become part of the Western Region, hence the LNWR (Crewe) frame, the BR starter, and the GWR outer home.

The last train to Ebbw Vale High Level organised by the SLS with "Coal Tank" and "Super D" on 5 January 1958 poses for passengers
photograph by N. Glover. In the lower picture can be seen Blaenavon High Level in 1956 — photograph by Mowat.

Westmoor Flag station was a private station where trains were stopped for the exclusive use of the owners. This 6 June 1960 photograph by Hugh Ballantyne shows a class 2, 2-6-0 No 46506 passing on the 12.42 pm Hereford to Three Cocks Jcn train. The line closed to passengers on 31 December 1962.

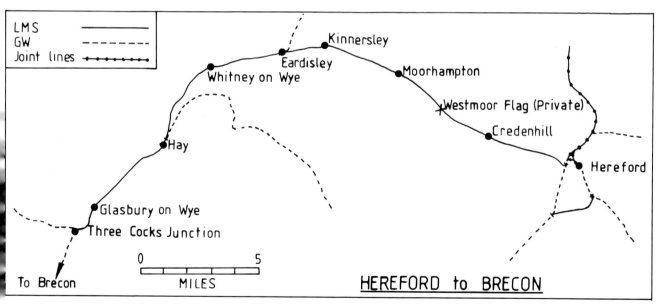

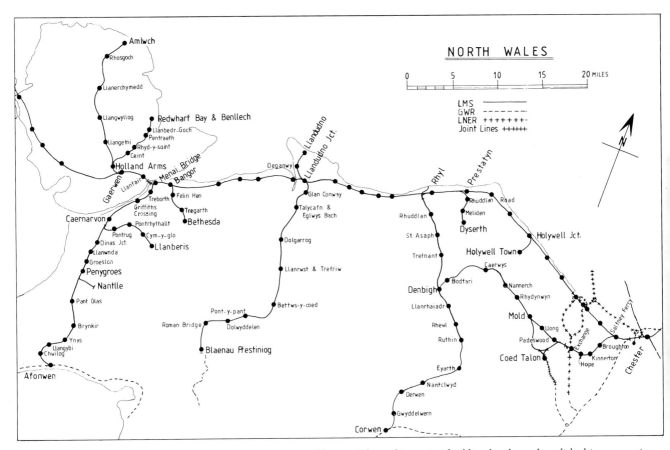

NORTH WALES

LMS	————			
GWR	– – – –			
LNER	++++++			
Joint Lines	+++++			

0   5   10   15   20 MILES

Amlwch
Rhosgoch
Llanerchymedd
Llangwyllog
Redwharf Bay & Benllech
Llanbedr Goch
Pentraeth
Rhyd-y-saint
Llangefni
Ceint
Holland Arms
Menai Bridge
Bangor
Caerwen
Llanfair
Treborth
Felin Hen
Griffiths Crossing
Tregarth
Bethesda
Caernarvon
Pontrhythallt
Pontrug
Cym-y-glo
Dinas Jct.
Llanberis
Llanwnda
Groeslon
Penygroes
Nantlle
Pant Glas
Brynkir
Ynys
Llangybi
Chwilog
Afonwen
Roman Bridge
Dolwyddelen
Pont-y-pant
Blaenau Ffestiniog
Bettws-y-coed
Llanrwst & Trefriw
Dolgarrog
Talycafn & Eglwys Bach
Glan Conway
Deganwy
Llandudno
Llandudno Jct.
Rhyl
Prestatyn
Rhuddlan Road
Rhuddlan
Meliden
Dyserth
St. Asaph
Holywell Jct.
Holywell Town
Trefnant
Caerwys
Nannerch
Rhydynwyn
Denbigh
Bodfari
Llanrhaiadr
Mold
Rhewl
Llong
Padeswood
Coed Talon
Ruthin
Exchange
Saltney Ferry
Broughton
Kinnerton
Hope
Chester
Eyarth
Nantclwyd
Derwen
Gwyddelwern
Corwen

Denbigh in April 1962, with a class 4 2-6-4T on a train to Chester. The gothic station building has been demolished in connection with a road widening scheme, but the goods shed on the right still remains.

Bethesda passenger station stands gaunt and isolated (above) in this photograph taken prior to closure to goods on 7 October 1963. Passenger trains were withdrawn on 3 December 1951. The LNWR opened the Prestatyn & Dyserth branch with a flourish in 1905 using the steam railmotors designed for the line. A LNWR publicity postcard of the period is illustrated (left). The terminus at Dyserth is illustrated (below right) with the goods warehouses and specially designed low platform. The passenger service ceased on 22 September 1930 but freight lasted well into BR days, the last train running in September 1973. Dyserth photograph by Lens of Sutton.

Llanrug on the LNWR Llanberis branch sees a class 4, 2-6-4 T No 42198 on August 1962. The line closed to all traffic on 7 September 1964. Photograph by R. Joanes.

Holywell Town with the push and pull train on 10 August 1953 – the line from Holywell Junction was only 1¾ miles long and had one intermediate halt called St Winefrides. The line closed to all traffic on 6 September 1954. Photograph by H.C. Casserley.

Present-day scenes on the Blaenau Ffestiniog branch, Bettws-y-Coed (above) and the brand new terminus at Blaenau Ffestiniog (below).

Ivatt class 2, 2-6-2T No 41224 with the Bangor train rests at Amlwch in steam days. The line is still used by freight trains although the buildings at Amlwch have been demolished, the passenger service having been withdrawn on 7 December 1964. Upper picture by Lens of Sutton. The lower photograph shows Red Wharf Bay station in pre-Grouping days with passengers waiting at the then new station opened in 1909.

APPENDIX — LMS STATIONS AND BUILDINGS

It is still possible to see evidence of the LMS building livery as many closed stations still retain traces of their former owners' paintwork. The LMS had by the mid 1930s established a standard formula for painting stations. Country buildings were painted brunswick green lower and cream upper, town stations were venetian red with cream or portland stone — more or less the London Midland Regional colour of BR. Less important buildings such as goods sheds were in dark brown with black — a very good example being the Northampton Bridge Street warehouses which can be seen today still in their LMS colours. Many country stations still sport the LMS green and cream on lines that have been closed for many years, where the buildings are still used. Some pre-Grouping examples can be viewed, such as the Midland at Oakworth on the Keighley & Worth Valley which is chocolate and cream with red doors and white on blue nameboards. The Lancashire & Yorkshire station livery can be seen at Hebden Bridge.

BIBLIOGRAPHY

Branch Line Index	G.C. Lewthwaite BLS 1963
British Branch Lines	H.A. Vallence Batsford 1965
The Lancashire & Yorkshire Railway	John Marshall D&C 1970
The North Staffordshire Railway	R. Christiansen & R.W. Miller D&C 1971
The Lowgill Branch	R.G. Weston Oakwood 1971
The Preston & Longridge Railway	N. Parker Oakwood 1972
The Furness Railway	R.W. Rush Oakwood 1973
A Regional History of Railways of Gt Britain—Vol 7	Rex Christiansen D&C 1973
The Churnet Valley Railway	R. Keys Moorland 1974
A Regional History of Railways of Gt Britain—Vol 8	David Joy D&C 1975
A Regional History of Railways of Gt Britain—Vol 9	Robin Leleux D&C 1976
A Guide to Closed Railways of Britain	N.J. Hill & A.O. McDougall BLS 1977
A Regional History of Railways of Gt Britain—Vol 10	Geoffrey Holt D&C 1978
The Banbury to Verney Junction Branch	Bill Simpson OPC 1978
The Prestatyn & Dyserth Railway	Trefor Thompson NCRA 1978
Walking Old Railways	C. Somerville D&C 1979
The Cheadle Railway	A. Baker Oakwood 1979
A Guide to the Steam Railways of Gt Britain	W. Awdry & C. Cook Pelham 1979
Discovering Lost Railways	F.G. Cockman Shire 1980
Preserved Locomotives	H.C. Casserley Ian Allan 1980
The Leek & Manifold Valley Light Railway	K. Turner D&C 1980
The Leek, Caldon & Waterhouses Railway	Basil Jeuda NSR Co 1980
Passengers No More	G. Daniels & L. Dench Ian Allan 1980
Rail Atlas of Britain & Ireland	S.K. Baker OPC 1980
A Walk Along the Tracks	Hunter Davies W&N 1982
LMS Miscellany	H.N. Twells OPC 1982
Sixpenny Switchback	P.M. White & J.W. Storer Pearson 1983
Oxford To Cambridge Railway—Vol I & II	Bill Simpson OPC 1983
Yorkshire Dales Railway	David Joy Dalesman 1983
Worth Valley Revival	KWVR KWVR 1983
The Northampton & Market Harborough Line	John Gough RCHS 1984
The Delph Donkey	M. & P. Fox M. & P. Fox 1984
The Bacup Branch	B.C. Lane LYRS 1985
The Garstang & Knott End Railway	R.W. Rush & M.R.C. Price Oakwood 1985
Leicester & Burton Branch Railway	H.N. Twells Trent Valley 1985
Shackestone, A Guide to Leicestershire's Steam Branch Line	SRS SRS 1985
Bradshaws July 1922 Railway Guide (reprint)	D&C D&C 1985
Railway Rights of Way	Rhys Ellis BLS 1985
The Coniston Railway	M. Andrews CRA 1985
The Merthyr, Tredegar & Abergavenny Railway	W.W. Tasker OPC 1986
LMS Branch Lines in North Wales	W.G. Rear Wild Swan 1986
The Skipton & Ilkley Line	F.W. Smith & D. Binns Wyvern 1986

also Branch Line News, Railway Magazine, Railway World, Steam Railway, Railway Observer, "The Wyvern", and BR public and working timetables.

ACKNOWLEDGEMENTS

The author and publisher would like to thank Rhys Ellis and John Langford for checking the manuscript, M.K. Pain for the maps and Derek Mercer for the photographic printing. M.A. Jose has provided tickets and technical advice.

INDEX